A Shetland Nature Diary

A Shetland Nature Diary

Joyce J. M. Gammack

Published by
The Shetland Times Ltd.,
Lerwick.
1996

To Douglas and Freya
with love

List of Colour Illustrations

Contents

Acknowledgments

I would like to express my gratitude to James R. Nicolson for his assistance and encouragement and to my husband, Douglas, for his unfailing support. I would also like to thank the designer, Richard Stafford, and the publications department of The Shetland Times Ltd.

Joyce J. M. Gammack,
1996

Foreword

Over the past 16 years Joyce Gammack's articles in *Shetland Life* have been among the most popular features of the magazine. She covers all aspects of Shetland wildlife, adding to our understanding of the common features and drawing our attention to the less obvious aspects which casual observers tend to overlook.

It is therefore fitting that Joyce, from her vast experience in the subject, should condense her wealth of knowledge into a "Shetland Nature Diary". The book takes the reader through the seasons, month by month, pointing out things to look for and explaining their importance in her own fluent yet painstaking style.

Unlike many writers on natural history Joyce has the ability to explain a phenomenon in words that anyone can understand. In this book she provides many memorable word pictures – like the rook with his "baggy trousers".

This book will be useful to visitors trying to learn as much as possible about Shetland in a short visit, while for those of us who live here it will give a fresh insight into the wonders of our wildlife, through the seasons, and make us appreciate an aspect of island life which we tend to take for granted.

James R. Nicolson,
Editor,
Shetland Life.

June, 1996.

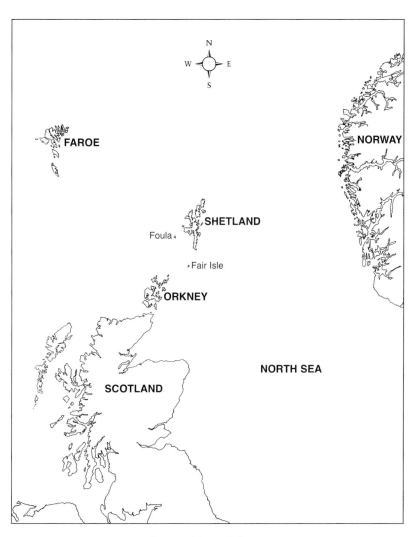

Location Map

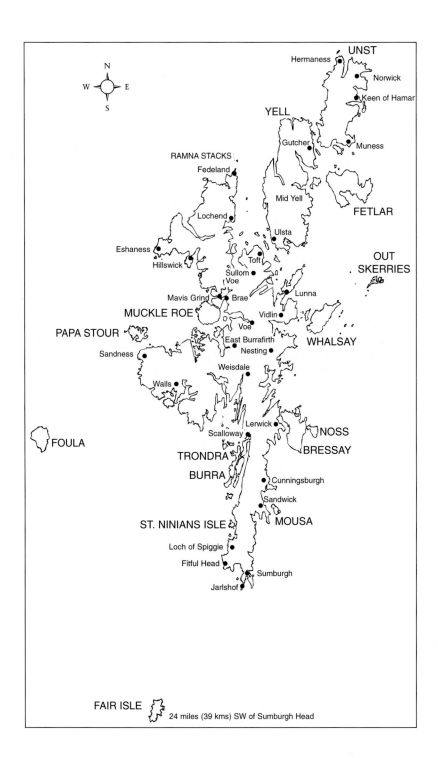

N

W   E

S

UNST

Hermaness ●

● Norwick

● Keen of Hamar

YELL

● Muness

Gutcher ●

RAMNA STACKS ●

Fedeland ●

Mid Yell

FETLAR

Lochend ●

Ulsta ●

Eshaness ●

OUT
SKERRIES

Hillswick ●

Toft ●

Sullom
Voe ●

Mavis Grind ● Brae ●

Lunna ●

MUCKLE ROE

Vidlin ●

PAPA STOUR

Voe ●

East Burrafirth ●

WHALSAY

Sandness ●

Nesting ●

Weisdale ●

Walls ●

Lerwick ●

NOSS

Scalloway ●

BRESSAY

TRONDRA

BURRA

Cunningsburgh ●

Sandwick ●

ST. NINIANS ISLE

MOUSA

Loch of Spiggie ●

Fitful Head ●

Sumburgh ●

Jarlshof ●

FOULA

FAIR ISLE

24 miles (39 kms) SW of Sumburgh Head

The Shetland Islands

Geographical Position

Viewed from the air, the Shetland Islands appear like the scattered pieces of an elongated puzzle strewn along a north-south axis of some 100 miles of sea between Unst and Fair Isle. The archipelago consists of over a hundred islands, washed on its eastern seaboard by the North Sea, fretted and fragmented along its western coasts by the Atlantic Ocean. Shetland is the most northerly part of the British Isles. Lerwick, the capital, at latitude 60° 9' N and longitude 1° 9' W is almost equidistant from Aberdeen on the Scottish mainland (211 miles/340km) and Bergen in Norway (230 miles/370km). The nearest island neighbours are the Orkney Islands, approximately 50 miles/80km to the south west, and the Faroe Islands 176 miles/284km north west.

The Larger Islands

The total land area of the islands is 567 miles²/468km² with the largest island, Mainland, comprising over 60% of the whole at 351 miles²/899km². Mainland, approximately 50 miles/80 km from north to south, is shaped roughly like a curved sword with its apex at North Roe and its tip at Sumburgh Head. The hilt is formed by the projecting bulge of West Mainland and the ragged promontory of Lunna Ness. Only 15 of the larger islands are inhabited; these include Papa Stour and the remoter island of Foula off the west coast, and Whalsay, Out Skerries and Bressay off the east coast. Fair Isle lies 24 miles/39km south west of Sumburgh Head, about mid-way between Orkney and Shetland. Yell, Fetlar and Unst are north of Mainland, whilst Trondra, Burra and Muckle Roe are connected to Mainland by bridges.

The Effect of the North Atlantic Drift

The Shetland Islands are at the same latitude as such locations as Cape Farewell in Greenland, St Petersburg in Russia, Stockholm in Sweden and Anchorage in Alaska – all of which experience temperatures considerably below freezing for prolonged periods during the winter. Low winter temperatures and long periods of cold snowy weather are a rarity in Shetland as the coastline is bathed by a warm sea water current, the North Atlantic Drift which is a branch of the Gulf Stream. The climate is thus temperate oceanic maritime with winter temperatures generally comparable to those in more southerly parts of Britain. The coldest month, February, only averages around 3°C (37.4°F). However, the islands lie in the path of depressions sweeping in from the North Atlantic so winters tend to be wet and windy with gales a predominant feature. A gale is defined as an average wind speed exceeding 39mph. The stormiest month is usually January and the prevailing wind direction is generally south west. The average wind speed throughout the year is 15-17mph and rainfall averages around 1143mm/45ins per year, with the highest amounts falling during the winter months.

Spring and Summer

During spring and summer prolonged periods of strong winds are unusual and rainfall decreases to around 63mm/2.5ins. Spring often comes late to Shetland, hampered by low temperatures and wet cold soils. Summers are generally cool, bright and breezy but there may be long settled spells of calm sunny weather. The warmest month is usually August when average temperatures reach 14°C (57°F) but sheltered spots may record much higher temperatures. Thunderstorms are uncommon, but sea fog can mar calm sunny days. Late spring and summer are characterised by the 'simmer dim' – long light evenings which are a consequence of Shetland's northerly position. On midsummer day, 21st June, the sun remains above the horizon for almost 19 hours and, on clear evenings, after sunset there is a prolonged period of bright twilight. This acts as some compensation for the long hours of darkness during winter – on midwinter's day the sun is only above the horizon for just over $5\frac{1}{2}$ hours.

Sea Temperatures

The sea temperatures around the Shetland Islands are tempered by the effect of the warm waters of the North Atlantic Drift and are also affected by the distribution of water masses around the islands. Temperatures range from 7°C during the coolest months of February and March, to 13°C during July and August.

Geology and Landscape

The geology of Shetland is extremely complex, forming an intricate skeleton which underlies all the other natural, and many of the man-made features of the islands. Features ranging from the distribution of cliff-nesting seabird colonies to the fertility of a freshwater loch are determined by geology. Habitats and their ecology are established by the structure of the rocks beneath.

Igneous rocks

All rocks on Earth originate in three main ways. *Igneous* rocks form in a molten state under the Earth's crust from a material called *magma* which consists of metallic silicates, water and gases at high temperatures. When the magma explodes through the surface in a violent eruption as lava, then extrusive igneous or *volcanic* rocks are formed. Volcanic lavas may be porous, e.g., pumice, or fine-grained such as basalt and andesite but their rapid cooling prevents crystal formation. Intrusive igneous rocks or *plutonic* rocks (named after Pluto, the Roman god of the underworld) are created when the magma cools and solidifies just before it reaches the surface. The molten rock may flow into areas of existing rock producing horizontal sills or vertical dykes, or it may consolidate into a molten mass or sheet. The slow heat loss allows crystals to form and, the slower the cooling, the larger the crystals. Typical examples of plutonic rocks found in Shetland include granite, diorite, gabbro and pegmatite. Igneous rocks are generally very hard and weather only gradually.

Sedimentary Rocks

All rocks weather and are eroded by a variety of physical agents – wind, ice, heating, cooling, chemicals from plant roots – and the products of erosion are then transported by wind, seas, rivers and glaciers. *Sedimentary* rocks are formed from these particles of pre-existing rock which settle out of solution and begin to accumulate underwater. As considerable pressure is exerted by the overlying layers, the particles are compacted and water is either squeezed out or is replaced by some other material as physical and chemical changes occur within the forming rock. Most sedimentary rocks show distinct layering or *bedding planes* caused by slight changes in the composition of the rock as it was laid down over thousands of years. Sedimentary rocks can contain fossils but there are few fossil beds in Shetland and these contain only the fragmentary remains of primitive armoured fish and ancient plants. Common sedimentary rocks in Shetland include sandstones, mudstones, shales, conglomerates and breccias. These last two rock types consist, respectively, of rounded pebbles or angular fragments embedded in a sedimentary matrix. Much of Shetland's sedimentary rocks are of Old Red Sandstone dating from around 350-400 million years ago. These rocks erode relatively easily.

Metamorphic Rocks

The third rock type, *metamorphic*, meaning ' to change shape' is created when pre-existing rocks are subjected to considerable heat and pressure. This can occur during phases of mountain building, faulting or volcanic activity. Elements within the rock either regroup into new minerals or reform into larger crystals of the existing minerals. The type of metamorphic rock formed depends on several factors such as the constituents of the original rock, the amount of pressure and the quantity of water involved. Examples of metamorphic rocks found in Shetland include schist, gneiss, crystalline limestone and serpentine. Some erode easily, e.g., schist and talc serpentine, whilst others are more resistant.

The Roots of Shetland

Some of the oldest rocks are over 2,000 million years old, dating from the Precambrian era. Occurring in the north west part of the Mainland, near Uyea and on the Ve Skerries, these rocks are the base of an ancient mountain chain. The Caledonian Mountain Belt once linked Norway and Scotland to parts of North America and Greenland, before being forced apart some 200 million years ago by the opening up of the Atlantic Ocean. Over millions of years the erosion products of the mountain chain underwent dramatic changes. Buried, faulted, deformed, re-crystallised, heated, cooled, sedimented, compacted, twisted, folded and uplifted they form much of the rocks of present Shetland.

Distribution of Rock Types

Geological complexity is difficult to summarise but the major areas of rock distribution, of significant importance in determining habitats, can be recognised. Running north-south through Shetland are several tear faults where blocks of rock have been violently displaced by movements of the Earth's crust, separating older rocks from younger formations. The largest, the Walls Boundary Fault, is probably an extension of the Great Glen Fault on the Scottish mainland.

The spine of Mainland Shetland is mostly composed of metamorphic schist and gneiss, non-porous rocks which enable the build-up of large tracts of nutrient-poor peaty soils. Inter-banded with these rocks are strips of crystalline limestone which erode to provide fertile brown soils, e.g., Fladdabister, South Nesting and the Tingwall valley. The backbone of schist and gneiss extends east to Whalsay and Out Skerries and north to Yell and the western parts of Unst and Fetlar. Much of the North Mainland, west of the fault line, consists of red granite and other igneous rocks. Ronas Hill at 453m/1,486ft is the highest point in Shetland and was formed from a large domed plutonic mass which almost reached the surface before crystallising. The rocks around Eshaness and on the island of Papa Stour were created by volcanic activity producing spectacular cliff scenery. In the West Mainland and on Foula, the Old Red Sandstone is interspersed with volcanic rocks. Along the eastern coast of Mainland, from just north of Lerwick to Sumburgh Head, an extensive band of Old Red Sandstone was deposited giving rise to fertile

4

agricultural soils. In places the sandstone is inter-banded with sections of crystalline limestone. These rocks also make up the islands of Bressay, Noss, Mousa and Fair Isle. The most complex geology is found in the eastern parts of Fetlar and Unst. Here a section of the ocean floor rode up over the land resulting in the formation of a variety of metamorphic rocks juxtaposed with existing granites, schists and gneisses. The most distinctive of these is the attractive greenish serpentine which, in its most altered form, is quarried in Unst as talc for industrial use.

The Ice Ages

Following the intricate geological processes which formed the rocky foundations of Shetland, Ice Ages sculpted the surface. Most evidence exists from the last Ice Age which began about 30,000 and ended around 12,000 years ago. As the ice advanced it accumulated loose rock and soil and acted like a gigantic sander smoothing, rounding and deepening the topography.

Shetland was peripheral to the huge ice sheets which depressed Scandinavia and Scotland. When the ice melted, these areas, free of their burden, began rising above sea level whilst the Shetland Islands started to slowly sink. The rising waters partially drowned the landscape, flooding river valleys and transforming them into long sea inlets or *voes,* surrounding hill tops to create islands, and surging up the cliffs along the outer coastline reducing their relative height. In the process, large quantities of till and loose bedrock were swept out into the sea and re-deposited in sheltered inlets as a series of sandy and shingly beaches, spits, bars and ayres – the classic features of a semi-drowned coastline.

Shetland Habitats

The islands are made up of a mosaic of different habitats which often merge into each other. These can be divided up into three main categories – coastal, terrestrial and freshwater/marsh. Within each are several distinct habitat types and gradations, all influenced by climate, the underlying rock and the effects of man. The first evidence of human occupation comes from ploughshare tip marks found at Sumburgh dated at around 3,200 BC. These early settlers began the process of modifying the landscape for their crops and animals which continues to the present day.

Coastal

The Shetland Coastline

Coastal habitats predominate. The involuted sea-infiltrated character of the coastline creates an extensive amount of coastal habitat, an estimated total length of around 1,450km/900 miles. The Shetland archipelago is surrounded by deep water – the 80m bathymetric contour line closely follows the shape of the islands. During autumn and winter storms nutrients are stirred up from the ocean depths. This produces high concentrations of nitrates and phosphates in surface waters which fuel spring blooms of phytoplankton. This explosion of microscopic plant life is feasted on by growing populations of zooplankton which, in turn, support substantial stocks of fish. The fish populations are the staple diet of seals, cetaceans and the thousands of seabirds which breed along the coastline and offshore islands during the summer months.

Sea Cliffs

Spectacular cliff scenery occurs, particularly along the north-west and western coasts which face the full fury of the Atlantic storms. At Hermaness in Unst rugged grey cliffs of schist and gneiss provide a dramatic backdrop, whilst Fetlar has blue-green banks of serpentine. The brooding dark basaltic cliffs and stacks of Eshaness contrast starkly with the surrounding aquamarine white-flecked seas. On Papa Stour the volcanic cliffs are composed of striking red rhyolite, whereas on Fair Isle, Foula, Noss, Bressay and Sumburgh Head there are the brownish-red tones of Old Red Sandstone. Ronas Voe and Muckle Roe have bastions of sparkling pinkish-red granite whilst the granitic cliffs of Westerwick are of a darker red.

The highest cliffs are on Foula – the Kame at 370m/1,214ft is the second highest cliff in Britain, only being surpassed by Conochair on St Kilda. On Mainland, the highest cliffs are at Fitful Head, 283m/929ft. Cliffs and sea are locked in a constant war of attrition. The sea is continually seeking out tiny fissures and zones of weakness in the rock; whittling out steep-sided gashes into *geos*, chiselling subterranean sea caves, isolating, carving and sculpting stacks, rock pillars and natural arches. The features which develop along a stretch of coastline depend on the type of rock and the degree of exposure.

Geology is also of paramount importance in determining the biological richness of the cliff habitat. Cliffs of igneous rock, such as granite, have steep sloping surfaces and erode very slowly. Only fulmars and, sometimes, small colonies of kittiwakes can find a foothold. The shallow top soil is unsuitable for burrow-nesters like puffins and only hardy pioneer plants like algae, lichens and mosses are capable of colonising the sheer inhospitable rock faces. In contrast, sedimentary and the softer forms of metamorphic rock can weather into a layered series of ledges, crevices and alcoves providing suitable nesting sites for cliff-nesting seabirds. Almost all the large seabird colonies are on Old Red Sandstone cliffs, except those on Unst and Fetlar where crumbly schist and gneiss provide a good alternative. However, not all sandstone cliffs support seabird colonies. It depends on the height of the cliff above sea level, the frequency of bedding planes in the rock and the angle of dip of the strata. Ideal conditions exist at the Noup of Noss where the almost horizontal strata has many unevenly eroded bedding planes creating a warren of ledges, cracks and hollows.

Rocky Shores

Along the shoreline rocky shores are dominant, their biological richness depending on the degree of exposure to wave action and the geology of the rocks. Where a rocky platform dips sharply into the sea, the shore is steep and narrow and the constant battering of incoming waves prevents colonisation by sedentary organisms. The steepness of the slope also reduces the available settlement area. The flatter and more irregular the shore profile, the more wave action is dissipated. Blanketing seaweed further lessens wave impact and protects inter-tidal organisms from predation and desiccation. The richest diversity of seashore life occurs where there are large boulders and rocky ridges providing a variety of niches. Sedimentary rocks form the richest of these habitats as they weather into rough-textured crannies and fissures. Erosion along the bedding planes can also create shallow rock pools. Gull species, oystercatcher and redshank feed along rocky shores whilst, in winter, turnstone and purple sandpiper occur. Wren and rock pipit forage along the foreshore and strandline, often accompanied by the ubiquitous starling. Offshore, kelp beds are the feeding grounds of eider, black guillemot *(tystie)*, seals and the elusive otter *(dratsie)*.

Sheltered Voes

Most of these tongue-like sea inlets, often stretching long fingers inland, are drowned river valleys. The longest is Sullom Voe which is over 13km/8 miles. Ronas Voe and Gloup Voe in Yell are the only true fjords. Gouged out by glaciation and steep-sided, these voes have deep water at the head and shallower contours near the mouth. Common seals favour the calmer waters of voes and many of these sea inlets offer good habitat for otters. They often contain small holms which hold nesting waders, gulls and terns and, in winter, the voes attract waterfowl such as eider, long-tailed duck, great northern diver, common and velvet scoter, tufted duck and red-breasted merganser.

Voe shorelines are very sheltered environments and are dominated by a yellow-brown seaweed, known as knotweed *(Ascophyllum nodosum)*, which is characteristic of these conditions. Most salt marshes in Shetland occur at the head of voes. Periodically flooded by salt water, these areas are colonised by specialised flowering plants. However salt marsh habitat in Shetland is fragmentary, poorly developed and limited in extent with a restricted range of species.

Shingle Beaches

This is the most barren of the coastal habitats due to the constant shifting and rolling of the pebbles. A shingle beach is composed of a mixture of stones and rounded pebbles of varying sizes (5-250mm/¼-10ins) in diameter. The more exposed a beach is to wave action, the more the shingle is differentially sorted with larger pebbles at the top sloping down to smaller ones on the lower shore. Powerful storm waves can create high level storm beaches piled with huge boulders as at Grutness in the South Mainland and the Grind of the Navir at Eshaness. The rate at which shingle is moved along a coastline is known as longshore drift and varies with wind strength, wave force and the slope of the beach. The complex shape of the Shetland coastline results in frequent changes in the direction of longshore drift. Sometimes a shingle spit starts to develop at right angles to the coast and may form an *ayre* or *tombolo* connecting an island to the shore. If it then bends back on itself the resulting barrier may cut off the head of a voe creating a brackish loch as at the Loch of Spiggie in the South Mainland and the Loch of Cliff in Unst.

In addition to being unstable surfaces for colonising organisms, shingle beaches are also very dry environments at low tide as the coarse nature of the materials prevents any upward movement of water by capillary action. However, beaches well above the average high tide level accumulate cast-up seaweed and other organic matter which decomposes into humus. Receiving sea spray, the stones retain mineral salts and create their own condensation thus providing a moist medium in which plants can grow. In Shetland extreme exposure of much of the foreshore limits the range of species, many shingle beaches only being colonised by quick-growing annuals such as orache *(Atriplex sp)*. At more sheltered sites, long-lived, deep-rooted perennials like sea campion and thrift become established. A specialist of this habitat is the rare attractive oyster plant *(Mertensia maritima)* now confined to only a handful of sites. Shingle ridges provide nesting sites for birds such as Arctic tern, oystercatcher, eider and ringed plover.

Sandy Beaches

There are over 100 sandy beaches of varying sizes but these account for only about 2% of the total length of coastline. The largest, approximately 1½km/1 mile long, is at Quendale in the South Mainland. The formation of these beaches depends on the availability of sand offshore and the presence of a raised platform onshore. Cliff foot sandy beaches are uncommon and most sandy stretches occur in sheltered bays and voes.

On average, about 50% of the sand components are crushed shells and sea urchin tests; the rest consists of siliceous particles washed out of glacial debris or weathered from local rocks. Many beaches reflect the local geology – red garnet sands in Yell, reddish-orange granite sands at Reawick in West Mainland, glittering mica sands in Unst. Few beaches have fully developed dune and machair systems – only Quendale exhibits all these features. Sand dunes are found at beaches such as St Ninians Isle, Scousburgh, Sumburgh and Grutness in South Mainland, Breckon and West Sandwick in Yell and Norwick in Unst.

The diversity of invertebrate life living in these beaches depends on the degree of exposure to wave action, the size of the sand particles and the amount of accumulated organic debris within the beach. Many organisms are deposit feeders, e.g., lugworms (*Arenicola marina*), which ingest particles of detritus in the sand or on the surface. Others are suspension feeders, e.g., razor shells (*Ensis s*p), filtering out edible particles from the tidal currents.

Mud flats form where high levels of organic material accumulate on a level beach. This is a habitat usually associated with river estuaries and, as a result, is rare in Shetland. Small areas of mud flat habitat are generally confined to the head of sheltered voes in the islands. The most important area is a shallow tidal basin covering an area of about 37 hectares/90 acres at the Pool of Virkie in the South Mainland. Mud flats have high concentrations of a tiny marine shell (*Hydrobia ulvae*) which are an important food source for small waders, such as ringed plover, and shelduck. Larger waders feed on bigger buried molluscs and worms. The Pool of Virkie is a site of prime importance particularly for wintering and migrating waders.

Terrestrial

Past Vegetation

Analysis of pollen grains, preserved in peaty soils, shows that the Shetland Islands once supported a scrub vegetation of trees and shrubs which reached its maximum cover about 7,500 years ago. The main tree species was birch with hazel, willow, rowan, juniper and poplar. It is probable that copses of birch and hazel grew on fertile soils to altitudes of 200m/656ft in sheltered valleys. Beneath these trees would have been an almost continuous field layer of tall grasses, flowering plants and ferns. In damper areas willow carr flourished, along with species such as common reed, royal fern and angelica. Around 3,400 BC the tree pollen shows a sharp decline along with a corresponding increase in the pollen of ling heather (*Calluna vulgaris*). At the same time evidence of ribwort plantain appears, a species closely associated with man.

These first settlers, Neolithic farmers, began clearing the scrub vegetation, using the trees as a source of fuel, to create pastures and fields for their livestock and crops. Grazing by domestic animals prevented tree and shrub regeneration, whilst the removal of tree cover encouraged the growth of ling and the subsequent formation of acidic peaty soils. This was exacerbated as the climate became colder and wetter. By the ninth century, when the Norsemen arrived in Shetland, only patches of scrub remained. Today, relict scrub woodland is reduced to scattered sites inaccessible to sheep – on sea cliffs, along steep-sided inland ravines and on small islands in freshwater lochs. The last remnants of our indigenous trees are mainly rowan, willow and wild rose with birch and hazel only recorded from a few locations.

Moorland

Acidic peaty soils have built up over much of the backbone of Shetland due to the non-porous nature of the predominantly schist and gneiss rock coupled with the grazing and burning of hill land for over 5,300 years. On the poorest soils large tracts of species-poor blanket bog have developed, dominated by a combination of ling heather, cotton grass *(Eriophorum angustifolium)*, deer grass *(Trichophorum cespitosum)* and *Sphagnum* mosses. Heather plants grow more slowly in Shetland than elsewhere due to the climate. On drier areas a mixture of bell heather (*Erica cineraria*) and crowberry *(Empetrum nigrum)* grows, along with around 18 species of herbaceous flowering plants including tormentil, heath-spotted orchid, heath milkwort, heath bedstraw and eyebright.

The moorlands are important for breeding birds such as great skua *(bonxie)*, Arctic skua, whimbrel, red-throated diver, golden plover, dunlin, Arctic tern and merlin. Other breeding moorland species include curlew, skylark, meadow pipit, wheatear, hooded crow and common gull. Merlin, the only regularly breeding bird of prey, are found in small numbers. Introduced red grouse are confined to hills on Mainland. Long-tailed field mice are found on moorland during the summer months but a general lack of abundance of rodent species restricts the occurrence of breeding birds of prey. Rabbits are found where moorland borders croft land, and mountain hares range throughout the hills of Mainland and also on the island of Vaila.

The serpentine and metagabbro soils of Unst and Fetlar support a distinctive base-rich dry heath vegetation with ling and bell heather co-dominant. Other species include thyme, beautiful St John's wort, purging flax, common violet, heath dog violet, tormentil, milkwort and bird's foot trefoil. These areas are particularly favoured by nesting whimbrel along with golden plover, ringed plover, dunlin and Arctic skua.

Hill Tops

The upland vegetation of Shetland is regarded as subarctic oceanic. The growing season at sea level in the islands is similar to that at Dalwhinnie, at an altitude of 350m/1,148ft, in the Scottish Highlands. Surrounding seas cause the air temperature to fall more rapidly with increasing altitude so that summer air temperatures at 305m/1,000ft in Shetland are equivalent to those at 762m/2,500ft in the Scottish mountains. Accordingly, Arctic-alpines, found at these heights in Scotland, occur at much lower altitudes in Shetland.

Fellfield

Fellfield is a term used to describe the areas of mountain-tundra debris soils which are common in places such as Norway, Greenland and Faroe. These unstable soils contain little organic matter and are composed of small angular stones. Exposed to alternate freezing and thawing, the stones move around forming characteristic stone stripes. In Shetland, fellfield is mainly found on the granite upper slopes of Ronas Hill and on serpentine soils in Unst, most notable the Keen of Hamar. It also occurs, to a lesser extent, on the sandstone summit of Sandness Hill, West Mainland, and on the Sneug in Foula. In some situations the fellfield is colonised by a low-growing mat of tough woolly hair moss (*Rhacomitrium lanuginosum*), a plant community known as Rhacomitrium heath.

Most of the summit of Ronas Hill is covered by a mixture of Rhacomitrium heath and an open vegetation dominated by viviparous fescue grass (*Festuca vivipara*) and three-leaved rush (*Juncus trifidus*). Arctic-alpine species growing on these granite debris soils include dwarf willow, alpine lady's mantle, trailing azalea, stiff sedge, spiked woodrush and alpine clubmoss.

The serpentine debris soils of Unst support a unique plant community, the best example of which occurs on the Keen of Hamar National Nature Reserve. Much of this low hill appears like a stony desert, interspersed with patches of thin, sandy heathland soils. Growing amongst the fragments of serpentine are small, low-growing plants including a national rarity, Norwegian sandwort (*Arenaria norvegica*), and an endemic sub-species, Shetland mouse-ear chickweed or Edmonston's chickweed (*Cerastium arcticum* ssp *edmonstonii*). Plants growing on the Keen exhibit unusual growth forms and are often hairier and have darker colouration than specimens of species found elsewhere. This may be due to a nutrient imbalance in the soil – there are high concentrations of nickel and chromium, but little phosphorus or nitrogen – or be caused by water stress as the stony soil drains very quickly. Other species found on the Keen include moss campion, hoary whitlow grass, northern rockcress, thrift, scurvy grass, sea plantain, stone bramble, early purple orchid, mountain everlasting, kidney vetch, spring squill, heath dog violet and thyme.

Grassland/Pasture

Unimproved grasslands have the highest wildlife value. The commonest occurrence is as maritime grassland on small islands and cliff tops. Traditionally managed hay meadows support a particularly rich variety of species and semi-improved grasslands are also important. These semi-improved grasslands are often on lightly or ungrazed abandoned croft sites which have been improved in the past by stone clearance, drainage, ploughing and manuring.

Common grassland species include red campion, bird's foot trefoil, meadow buttercup, tufted vetch, meadow vetchling, angelica, yarrow, hogweed, sheep's bit, devils-bit, yellow rattle, mouse-ear chickweed, eyebright and clover. Species-rich grassland often abuts cultivated strips in agricultural areas and turns summer roadside verges into a riot of colour. Breeding birds include oystercatcher, curlew, lapwing, wheatear, skylark and meadow pipit. Rabbit, field mouse, stoat and hedgehog are also found in grassland habitats.

Wet Meadow

On the wetter margins of croft land and along roadside ditches a wild flower and sedge-rich vegetation occurs. These wet meadows are typically left untouched until autumn and then cut for hay. In their full glory they are one of the most beautiful of all grassland habitats supporting such colourful species as yellow iris, the golden masses of marsh marigold, yellow-orange swathes of mimulus, the deep purples of northern fen orchid, pink splashes of ragged robin, creamy-white clouds of meadowsweet and the delicate, golden-centred blues of forget-me-not. Curlew, snipe and mallard often nest in these areas. The mammals associated with grassland also occur as may common frogs.

Agricultural Land

Cultivated land in Shetland is confined to coastal areas and a few valley bottoms. Agriculture is largely based around crofts or small holdings although there are several larger farms in the more fertile areas. A typical croft consists of a low dwellinghouse and outbuildings, often enclosed by a stone wall and shrubs. Surrounding the buildings are cultivated fields or rigs leading on to grassland. Beyond the cultivated areas is the hill land or moorland where crofters share common grazing and peat rights.

The croft buildings provide nesting sites for birds such as house sparrow, blackbird, wren and starling. In addition, they frequently shelter those species of mammal closely associated with man – the house mouse and brown rat. The crofting system is mainly dependent on sheep rearing although cattle are kept on better soils. The Shetland sheep is a small tough animal, capable of grazing on nutrient-poor moorland vegetation for much of the year. Traditionally crops are grown to feed livestock and for home consumption.

Grass, in the form of hay or silage, is the most common fodder crop along with swedes and Shetland cabbage. Turnips, potatoes and carrots are also cultivated. In winter crop fields provide valuable shelter for migrants. As hay meadows are not harvested until after the breeding season many of the breeding bird species found on grassland can nest there. In autumn the cleared fields attract foraging rock dove, twite, starling, gulls and waders. Hay stacks or *desses* often harbour long-tailed field mice and hedgehogs which move into agricultural land as the weather grows colder. In some parts of the islands parts of moorland and rough pasture have been reclaimed by fencing, fertilising and re-seeding. Some of these fields are particularly attractive to migrant and wintering geese.

Plantations / Gardens

The keynote to successful tree growing in Shetland is the provision of shelter from prevailing winds and grazing animals, and also in choosing appropriate hardy species. The most common species in plantations and private gardens are sycamore, elder and willow. Experimental Forestry Commission plots, planted in the 1950s, contain coniferous trees such as sitka spruce, lodgepole pine, mountain pine and Japanese larch. Many former lairds' houses have walled gardens containing sizeable trees. The most extensive area of planted woodland (about 3.3 hectares/8 acres) is in the sheltered fertile valley of Kergord. In recent years, tree planting for amenity value and shelter belts has been encouraged. Additional recommended species include birch, aspen, hazel, whitebeam, alder and elm. Shrubs such as honeysuckle, rose (*Rosa rugosa*), flowering currant and fuschia are popular and flourish in sheltered conditions

Even small areas of woodland habitat act as a mecca for migrant birds, providing life-giving shelter and sources of food. After a good 'fall' these areas are alive with species such as goldcrest, robin, blackcap, redstart, blackbird, song thrush, warblers, flycatchers and finches. Shetland's plantations also provide nest sites for a few regularly breeding woodland species. A colony of rooks has become established at Kergord. Collared doves breed mainly in Lerwick and Scalloway and a few pairs of wood pigeon also breed in Shetland. Long-eared owls and occasional small woodland birds, e.g., great tit, greenfinch, robin, over-winter in plantations and gardens.

Freshwater/ Marshes

An aerial view of Shetland reveals an intricate patchwork of small lochs, particularly in the West and North Mainland. Out of an approximate 2,500 freshwater bodies about 1,000 were created by glaciers creating out basins in the rock.

The ecology of a freshwater loch is determined by the nutrient content of the surrounding soils which, in turn, depends on the geology of the rocks. Freshwaters are generally classified by their alkalinity, usually expressed as the amount of dissolved calcium carbonate (Ca Co^3) in parts per million (ppm). Where the alkalinity is high the water is rich in nutrients and supports a rich diversity of plant and animal life. As alkalinity decreases, the water becomes more acidic and the range and quantity of flora and fauna declines correspondingly. This is also known as *trophic status* (from a Greek word meaning 'feeding'). The most common types of lochs in Shetland are acidic, *oligotrophic* (about 10 ppm Ca CO^3) and *dystrophic* (< 10 ppm Ca CO^3) water bodies on nutrient-poor soils.

Hill Lochs

Dystrophic lochs are found in areas where thick layers of blanket peat have accumulated. They are typically small and shallow with peat-stained waters which limit light penetration and, thus, the growth of aquatic plants. Nutrient content and biological productivity is very low and the characteristic vegetation is submerged *Sphagnum* moss and bulbous rush. Where the shoreline is sheltered, emergent species such as bottle sedge, cotton grass and bog bean occur. These sombre, soft-edged, peaty pools are favoured nesting sites for red-throated divers and bathing places for great skuas. Moorland pools may also attract kittiwakes which commute from nearby sea cliffs to collect wet mud for nest building. Whilst tufted duck and eider may nest on the shores of larger dystrophic lochs.

Oligotrophic lochs occur where the rocks are predominantly granite, schist and gneiss and are typically larger and deeper than dystrophic water bodies. Their waters are clear and peat-free with stony bottoms. Like dystrophic lochs, the nutrient concentration and biological productivity are low. Many of these crystal-clear lochs are on the glacially-eroded granite plateau of North Roe. The flora is restricted to a narrow, peripheral band of vegetation and is similar to that of dystrophic lochs, with the addition of common quillwort and water lobelia. Other species growing on the gravelly shores include common spike rush, jointed rush and shoreweed. These lochs support few species of aquatic invertebrates. However, brown trout are typical species as they require stony areas for spawning and thrive in cool, oxygen-rich waters. Arctic terns may nest along the shores and the loch waters often attract bathing gulls and skuas.

Lochs on Agricultural Land

In parts of Shetland where there are fertile brown soils, or along sandy coastlines, nutrient-rich *eutrophic* lochs occur (> 10 ppm Ca CO_3). The aquatic flora includes species such as amphibious bistort, mares tail, water milfoil, stonewort and various species of pondweed. These lochs support a more varied invertebrate fauna with water beetles, water boatmen, water snails and aquatic insect larvae. The richest of these lochs is at Hillwell in the South Mainland, situated on calcareous shell sand near Quendale Bay. The loch provides both shelter and winter feeding for waterfowl like shoveler, tufted duck, teal, shelduck, moorhen, coot and whooper swan whilst the surrounding marshes are favoured by waders such as lapwing, curlew and snipe. The nearby Loch of Spiggie is an RSPB (Royal Society for the Protection of Birds) reserve and holds large numbers of waterfowl during the winter months, particularly whooper swans.

Marshes

Many of the plant species found in wet meadow habitats also occur on marshy fens. Ungrazed fens are rare but, where they occur, the range of species is diverse including bottle sedge, bog bean, marsh cinquefoil, amphibious bistort, jointed rush, spike rush, marsh marigold, lesser spearwort, yellow iris, ragged robin, eyebright, yellow rattle, lady's smock, horsetails and grasses. Marshy areas attract breeding waterfowl and waders. The rare red-necked phalarope, an Arctic wader, only breeds in marshy areas on the island of Fetlar. Lochs in these habitats are often frequented by otters.

Burns and Streams

Shetland has no river systems and most of the burns have nutrient-poor waters flowing over gravelly or boulder beds. These support typical swift-current invertebrates which require well-oxygenated water such as stonefly, mayfly and caddisfly larvae. Where streams are slower moving, plant species like water starwort, marsh marigold, mimulus, meadowsweet, water forget-me-not, water mint and pondweeds become established. Well-vegetated burns, streams and ditches provide valuable cover for breeding and over-wintering waterfowl and migrant species. Burns and streams are also important as route-ways linking wet areas, lochs and the sea. They are particularly important for otters. Although otters in Shetland are almost completely marine they require access to freshwater to wash the salt from their fur, an essential part of coat maintenance.

Shetland Wildlife

The further an island group is from the mainland, the less the species diversity. Many species, common in northern Scotland, are absent from Shetland or at the extreme northerly end of their range. Genetic isolation of Shetland populations has produced local races or *sub-species* of several species. These races have evolved distinctive characteristics as compared with members of the same species elsewhere.

Birds

Shetland's bird interest can be divided into four main categories - seabirds, other breeding species, migrants and winter visitors.

Seabirds

Shetland is justly famous for its huge seabird populations. The islands are situated near the edge of the continental shelf. Here a branch of the westerly North Atlantic Drift, flowing through the Fair Isle Channel into the North Sea, meets a current of coastal water, enriched by land drainage, which is travelling up the north east coast of Britain. The convergence of these currents causes nutrients to be brought up from the depths of the sea during winter storms. This rich mineral soup results in extensive growths of plankton which power a rich marine ecosystem.

Of the 24 species of breeding seabirds in the British Isles, 21 breed in Shetland. Most are summer visitors, coming back in their thousands each spring to start their breeding season and take advantage of the fish stocks around the islands. The largest accessible seabird colonies are found at Hermaness NNR (National RSPB Nature Reserve) Unst, North Fetlar RSPB reserve, Noss NNR, Sumburgh Head RSPB reserve, Foula and Fair Isle. Seabird colonies which are NNRs cover an area of 1293.3 hectares/3,195.7 acres, and those designated as SSSIs (Sites of Special Scientific Interest) cover a total area of 3858.7 hectares/9534.7 acres.

Common species which breed on the sea cliffs include fulmar, shag, puffin, razorbill, guillemot, black guillemot, kittiwake, herring gull and great black-backed gull. Gannet colonies are found at Hermaness, Noss, Foula and Fair Isle. Arctic tern and common gull breed along the shores and on moorland. Great and Arctic skuas also nest on the moorland. The cormorant population is small and breeding sites are mainly confined to the west coast of the islands. Storm petrel are found at several localities, most notably on the island of Mousa, whilst small numbers of Manx shearwater and the rare Leach's petrel are confined to a few sites. Small populations of black-headed gull nest on marshes and small islands. Lesser black-backed gull and common tern also breed in Shetland but numbers are declining.

Many of the seabird populations are of national and international importance. The most significant is the number of great skuas which comprises 75% of the British population and 45% of those found in the northern hemisphere.

Other important populations, expressed in terms of % of the British population are:-

Arctic Skua	61%
Fulmar	35%
Black Guillemot	30%
Shag	25%

Other Breeding Species

About 44 species are recorded as regular breeders. Most important of these are Arctic species breeding at the southern extremities of their range – whimbrel, red-throated diver and red-necked phalarope. The Shetland populations of these species make up, 95% (whimbrel) and 40-60% (red-throated diver) of the British population. Almost the entire British red-necked phalarope population breeds on Fetlar. Large tracts of moorland and rough pasture provide nesting habitat for a variety of wader species including curlew, oystercatcher, snipe, lapwing, golden plover, dunlin and ringed plover. However, the lack of shrub and tree cover limits the occurrence of small passerines. Common breeding small birds include starling, blackbird, meadow pipit, rock pipit, wren, skylark, wheatear, twite and house sparrow. Other breeding species which occur widely are eider, mallard, red-breasted merganser, rock dove, hooded crow and raven.

Migrants

The Shetland Islands are located at the inter-section of two imaginary triangles. One extends from Shetland, at its northerly apex, to the south coast of Britain including the British Isles and Ireland; the other takes in Iceland, Faroe, the Arctic Circle and Western Scandinavia with the Shetland Islands at its southerly apex. The islands are therefore at the centre of east-west, north-south migration routes and represent a very important 'stepping stone' for migrant birds. The appearance of migrant species in both spring and autumn is dependent on prevailing weather systems during these months. Spectacular 'falls' generally occur when weather fronts come in from the south east.

Spring migrants start passing through in late March and continue into June, with a few species occurring into July. Regular migrants include blackbirds, thrushes, goldcrests, redstarts, flycatchers, warblers, pipits, wheatears and whinchats. Rarer species such as bluethroat, wryneck, golden oriole, ortolan bunting and great grey shrike may appear, along with very rare species from America, Europe and Asia.

Autumn migration commences in mid July and continues until about late October. First to arrive are waders returning from breeding in the Arctic. By August the first of the passerines appear, with the greatest numbers and diversity of species generally occurring in September. Regular autumn rarities include species such as lanceolated, barred and yellow-browed warbler. September and October are also the months when waterfowl and geese are migrating.

Winter Visitors

Many species from the Arctic regularly over-winter in the islands, escaping the severe conditions further north. Larger lochs support species such as whooper swan, goldeneye, pochard, mallard, tufted duck and wigeon. Offshore, long-tailed duck, little auk and great northern diver occur, with small numbers of Slavonian grebe in sheltered voes. Along the coast are foraging turnstone and purple sandpiper. Glaucous and Iceland gulls are regular winter visitors, occasionally joined by rarer northerly gull species. Flocks of snow bunting also over-winter whilst fieldfare and redwing may be found in small numbers.

Mammals

This category can be divided into sea-living mammals regularly observed around the Shetland coastline, and land mammals, almost all of which were introduced to the islands by man.

Sea Mammals

Grey and common seals breed around the coastline of Shetland with estimated populations, respectively, of 3,500 and 4,780. The grey seal population only represents 4% of the British population whilst the Shetland common seal population makes up around 19% of the common seals in Britain. Common seals pup in June/July and greys in late October/November. Vagrant seals from the Arctic, such as harp, ringed and bearded seals, along with the occasional walrus, have been recorded.

The surrounding rich waters provide good feeding grounds for cetaceans. The larger whales occur in deeper waters beyond the continental shelf, but the proximity of these areas to the islands mean that sightings are not uncommon. Rorquhals such as sei, minke and humpback whales have been observed recently. Of the toothed whales, there have been offshore sightings of sperm whales and strandings of carcasses, whilst pods of killer whales are regular visitors. The commonest of the smallest cetaceans is the common or harbour porpoise and Atlantic white-sided, common and Risso's dolphins are also recorded on a regular basis. Another of the smaller cetaceans, the long-finned pilot whale or *caa'in whale* was driven or 'caa'd' ashore by small boats in the eighteenth and nineteenth centuries and slaughtered for its blubber. At present around 20 species of cetaceans have been recorded in Shetland waters.

Land Mammals

There are only eight species of land mammals – hedgehog, stoat, otter, mountain hare, rabbit, long-tailed fieldmouse, house mouse and brown rat. Brown hares and black rats were introduced earlier this century but have since died out. Several species of vagrant bats have been recorded, the commonest wanderer being the pipistrelle. There are also breeding feral populations of domesticated ferrets and polecat-ferrets.

All land mammals, with the possible exception of the otter, were brought to the islands by man. The long-tailed fieldmouse and the house mouse populations show genetic affinities with these species in Norway and are therefore thought to have arrived with the Vikings in the 9th century. Brown rats probably arrived in trading ships at a later date. Stoats and rabbits were introduced around the seventeenth century whilst the hedgehog and mountain hare were nineteenth and twentieth century introductions. Most of the mammal species are widespread on the Mainland and some also occur on the larger islands. The otter population, estimated at 850-1,100, is of international importance.

Amphibians and Fish

Amphibians

This group is not native to Shetland. Both common frogs and toads have been introduced but only the frogs have survived. Common frogs are now widespread throughout Mainland and are also found on islands such as Yell, Unst and Bressay.

Freshwater Fish

Brown trout are common in most of the Shetland lochs. Spawning sea trout return during autumn to larger burns and lochs close to the sea. Salmon are only found in the largest burns and escapees from fish farms may also occur. Rainbow trout have been introduced experimentally into some angling lochs but are not very successful. The deep waters of the Loch of Girlsta support a population of char. Eels and three-spined stickleback are also common in burns and lochs throughout the islands.

Marine Fish

Shetland has a long history of fishing. The main commercial pelagic, or surface-shoaling, species are herring and mackerel. Sand-eels are also fished industrially for processing into fish meal but this fishery is carefully controlled. Sand-eels are a vital food item in the diet of seabirds. Commercially important demersal, bottom-dwelling, species include cod, haddock, whiting and monkfish. Other demersal species, common in Shetland waters, are ling, skate and coalfish or *saithe*.

Invertebrates

Marine Life

The marine environment is rich in invertebrates with several Arctic species occurring. The pollution-free waters enable the formation of thriving underwater communities which include species of sponges, hydroids, sea anemones, echinoderms, tube-worms, crustacea, molluscs and sea squirts. Sheltered rocky shores support typical inter-tidal fauna such as beadlet sea anemone, shore crab, tube-worms, ragworms, scaleworms, limpets, winkles, whelks, starfish, sea urchins, butterfish and rockling.

Terrestrial Invertebrates

The isolated position of Shetland and its northerly location limits both the number of invertebrate groups and the species diversity within these. Lepidoptera (butterflies and moths) have received the most attention. The total number of recorded species to date is over 200. Many are migrants, occurring only at certain times of year. Twelve species of butterflies have been observed but only the large white is resident.

Plant Life

Over 820 species of flowering plants and ferns have been recorded. However, excluding casuals, garden escapees and plants introduced by agricultural agencies, the list is about 568 species. Although the flora is restricted compared to that of mainland Britain, many species which are becoming rare elsewhere are still common in Shetland due to the continuation of many traditional agricultural practices.

After sunset, Yell.

Amazing sky, Cunningsburgh.

Old red sandstone cliffs, Fair Isle.

Rhydlite cliffs, Papa Stour.

Breaking waves, near Fitful Head.

Norwick beach, Unst.

Oyster plant.

Edible sea urchin.

—— IN ——

January

See winter comes to rule the varied year.

James Thompson

J anuary was dedicated by the Romans to the double-headed god, Janus, who was believed to be present at every gate, door and passage-way. Therefore the first month of the year, the passageway into the new year, bears his name. In Shetland, this first month is generally rather cold and grey. Polar air masses dominate the weather and gales, sometimes culminating in storm force winds, are frequent. However calm sunny cold spells can transform the islands - the crystal-like purity of a winter's day being almost tangible. Throughout the month the days are slowly, almost imperceptibly, beginning to lengthen.

January is not the most obvious month for visiting the seabird cliffs and yet these sombre bastions of rock are starting to show signs of the turning of the year. On still winter mornings a familiar chorus of growling 'aars' echoes along the cliffs. Clustered at the foot, like black and white beads, are a huddle of common guillemots. They are regular visitors during spells of calm weather throughout the winter. Also at the base of the cliffs, groups of resident shags gather on flat seaweed-covered rocks. By the end of the month they will be starting to sprout their recurved rather comical crests in readiness for the breeding season.

Like grey ghosts, fulmars are wheeling over the cliff tops. Breeding pairs are already ensconced at nest sites, defending their chosen niche with loud cackling calls, although the eggs will not be laid until May. Fulmars are long-lived seabirds with a probable life span of fifty years so they can afford to delay breeding until they are at least eight years old. After fledging, the young birds roam the North Atlantic for about five years before returning to prospect for a future mate and nest site. Superbly adapted gliders, fulmars belong to the same group as albatrosses. When gliding the slender narrow wings are held in a stiff slightly down-curved position, whilst the webbed feet are used for steering and making slight flight adjustments. The large eyes are set in deep grooves amongst the facial feathers thus increasing streamlining.

Offshore, grey wintry seas can look uninviting but a closer look may reveal a flotilla of eider or long-tailed duck. Eider are resident in the islands but long-tailed duck are winter visitors, having a

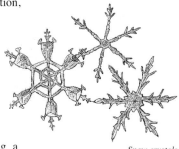

Snow crystals

21

circumpolar breeding distribution on the Arctic tundra. This elegant sea-duck appears almost too fragile to withstand the surging seas but it is a tough survivor. The adult males, beautifully marked in black and white, sport elongated tail streamers, whilst the brown and white females and juvenile birds lack these distinctive plumes. The Shetland name is the *calloo* on account of its loud resonant yodelling call. Long-tailed ducks winter in voes and in shallow waters offshore where they feed on a wide range of plants and animals, especially mussels, cockles and winkles.

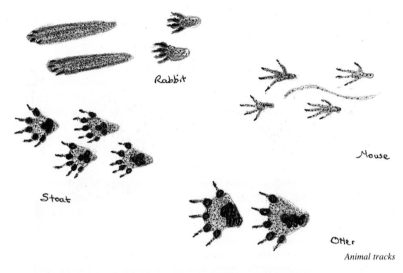

Animal tracks

Great northern divers may also be observed offshore. An estimated 300 birds from Greenland and Iceland winter around Shetland. Great northerns are thick-necked bulky-looking birds with stout heavy bills. In winter plumage they are dark above and white below. A few non-breeders remain throughout the summer, moulting into the striking chequer-board upperparts, white underparts, glossy black head and neck with striped part-collars.

Rocky shorelines attract foraging herring and great black-backed gulls. These species remain in the islands throughout the year also scavenging around harbours, fish factories and built-up areas. A walk along the shore often disturbs a redshank which quickly takes flight uttering shrill yelps of alarm. The strandline, depository for man-made and natural flotsam and jetsam, hosts flocks of the ubiquitous starling, noisily squabbling over the spoils. On the upper shore, tiny Shetland wrens creep amongst the boulders in their quest for insects whilst rock pipits flit around the lichen-encrusted rocks.

The weed-blanketed rocks attract wintering turnstone and purple sandpiper from the Arctic. Turnstones often appear to be in perpetual motion as they scurry around the strandline or over the rocks, flicking over stones and busily tweeking at fronds of seaweed in their assiduous search for small invertebrates. In flight the predominant impression is of a black and white wader but the winter plumage is actually grey-brown and white with contrasting orange legs.

Purple sandpipers are smaller, less conspicuous and less common than turnstone. They forage on seaweed-covered rocks close to the edge of the sea, feeding on small animals exposed by the falling tide. Dumpy in appearance with dark brownish upperparts and lighter underparts, they display a white wing-bar in flight. The slightly down-curved bill is brownish-orange and the legs are yellow. The name is a bit of misnomer although birds in summer plumage have a faint purple sheen on the scapular feathers.

Along some stretches of coastline grey herons stand hunched and motionless at the water's edge with dagger-like bills poised. These herons come from Scandinavia, most from Norway, where marshes and rivers often freeze in winter. They spend the winter months in Shetland around rocky shorelines, lochs and voes, feeding mainly on eels and other fish. Herons have a special adaptation for keeping their feathers clean and free of fish scales and slime. A tract of feathers growing on the breast and flanks produce a crumbly powdery material when touched by the beak. This powder down is spread over any fishy debris on the feathers thus soaking it up. Comb-like claws on the feet are then used to scrape off the mixture. In flight a heron is unmistakable, with a wing span of up to 1.95m/76 ins, head drawn back into the shoulders, and long projecting legs and feet. These large birds are often mobbed by gulls and crows when they take to the air.

Goose barnacle

An overnight snowfall followed by a calm cold morning provides a good opportunity to check on the comings and goings of the local mammal populations. Animal tracks show up best in fresh snow; later in the day the sun may cause a partial melt which distorts the prints. Tracks can often be found alongside walls and at the edges of fields. The prints of stoats and ferrets show the rather pointed imprints of five toes with sharp claw marks on both fore and hind feet. Rats and mice tracks have four toes on the forefeet and five toes on the hindfeet with the outside toes set back on the pads. There may also be a trace left by the tail. Rabbit and hare tracks are large and conspicuous, the larger four-toed hind tracks appearing in front of the five-toed fore tracks as the animal hops through the snow. Mountain hare tracks are larger than that of rabbits, and more indistinct due to the hairy pads on the underside of the toes. Dog prints have four toe prints with blunt claws and a triangular pad mark whilst the tracks of a cat are also four-toed but show no claw marks as the claws are retracted.

Otter tracks display a twisted pad with five pointed toes, armed with sharp claws, on all four feet and the drag marks of the tail may show up. Despite the short days this is a good time of year to observe otters. The lower light intensities may encourage these mammals to come nearer to human habitation and even take up residence. A friend, returning to Shetland from his Christmas break discovered that a female otter and three cubs were living in his peat shed. Despite human comings and goings the otter family continued to enjoy the comforts of their unusual home for several months.

January storms often throw up interesting shells. Along beaches the shells of large offshore bivalves, such as those of the horse mussel are common. These bluish-purple shells average a length of around 13 cm/5 ins and are often encrusted with barnacles and keel worms. The thick valves of the northern bivalve, *Arctica islandica,* are an interesting find. The large heavy shells are oval or circular with similar valves, and are covered in a dark leathery coating. On the inner surface of the shells the indentations of the powerful adductor muscles, which hold the valves closed, can be clearly seen. Another large bivalve, the common otter shell, reaches a length of 14 cm/5½ ins. The shell is shaped like an elongated oval and is usually yellowish-white or pinky-brown in colour. The large creamy coiled shells of common whelks, *Buccinium undatum,* are also frequently washed up.

Large pieces of wood which have been adrift for some time may harbour interesting passengers such as goose barnacles. These are crustaceans related to the common acorn barnacles of rocky shores. Five bluish-white plates with narrow blackish edges make up a triangular-shaped shell about 5 cm/2 ins in length. Attached to the shells are dark retractable stalks approximately 15 cm/6 ins. The planktonic larvae settle on large floating objects, often ship keels, and grow into sedentary adults. Goose barnacles feed by protruding their hair-fringed legs from the shell and sieving out phytoplankton cells. In medieval times it was believed that these barnacles were an immature stage in the life of the barnacle goose. This myth was used to explain the mystery of migration, as barnacle geese breed in the Arctic and winter in Britain. The black stalk was the goose's neck and the plates the wings. These 'young geese' then hung by their beaks from a 'barnacle tree' in the rotting hulls of old ships until they were ready to fly!

At this time of year few insects will be seen. Many overwinter in sheltered crevices and within tussocks of grass. At the base of the tussock the stems are packed tightly together. Tiny insects push their way down through the stalks into the relatively mild and dry conditions at the centre of the tussock. Here they are protected from the worst of the winter weather as the tussock generates its own micro-climate.

Beetles and other invertebrates such as woodlice seek out cracks in walls, creep under stones or enter the dead hollow stems of larger plants such as hogweed and angelica. The two commonest and most widespread species of woodlouse are the rough woodlouse, *Porcellio scaber*, and the shiny woodlouse, *Oniscus asellus*, both reaching lengths of about 16 mm/0.6 in. *Porcellio* is typically a dark matt grey with prominent tubercles and has the last section of the antennae divided into two small segments. It can tolerate drier habitats than *Oniscus*. Usually shiny grey in colour with lighter patches, *Oniscus* has three segments on the last section of its antennae. Woodlice are crustaceans and lack the waterproof covering

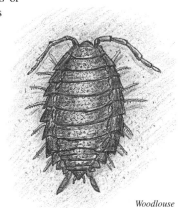

Woodlouse

24

which insects have developed. Accordingly, they must congregate in damp, sheltered places to keep their bodies moist. Beneath the abdomen are five pairs of leaf-like flaps which act as gills but these can only absorb oxygen when surrounded by a thin film of moisture. Woodlice instinctively move away from light, dry conditions into dark, damp areas and navigate into narrow crevices and under stones by slowing down and stopping moving when both upper and lower sides of the body are in contact with surfaces. Nine species have been recorded in Shetland.

At this time of year, when there a few plants flowering, lichens are more conspicuous. A lichen consists of a fungus and an alga which live in symbiosis ie to the mutual benefit of both organisms. The fungus gives the lichen its shape and protects the alga; the alga photosynthesises producing carbohydrates for the partnership. The fungus is the dominant organism but it can only survive when it is in contact with the appropriate alga. Lichens have no roots and can therefore colonise bare rock, obtaining necessary nutrients and minerals by absorption of water and gases through the upper surface. This makes them extremely sensitive to air-borne pollution and many only flourish in clean moist environments like Shetland. They are long-lived organisms only growing very slowly.

One of the commonest coastal lichens is *Xanthoria parietina* which grows in vivid leafy orange-yellow patches on rocks, stones and walls, especially where the substrate has been enriched by bird or animal faeces. Other species of coastal lichens, belonging to the genus *Caloplaca,* also form orangy crust-like growths on rocks. Crabs-eye lichen, *Ochrolechia parella* has a whitish-grey crust with distinctive raised discs. Lichens belonging to the genus *Ramalina,* often known as sea ivory, grow as tufts of tough, yellowish-grey, strap-shaped fronds. Another distinctive species, *Rhizocarpon geographicum,* is common on hard smooth siliceous rocks where it forms yellow-green patches delineated with thin black lines, like the continents on a map.

On the moorland the bright red spore capsules of *Cladonia* lichens provide tiny cheerful splashes of winter colour. *Cladonia floerkeana,* sometimes known as devil's matchsticks, has short scaly stalks with fiery scarlet heads. It favours bare patches of soil beneath old clumps of heather. *Cladonia coccifera* forms patches of greyish-yellow, warty stalks which bear exquisite miniature 'pixie cups' rimmed with tiny beads of bright red. These red structures are the spore-bearing parts of the fungus.

By the end of January signs of spring growth are starting to appear. Tree buds are swelling on the bare branches and bulb shoots are showing through. Although the Shetland winter is not yet over, these signs are a welcome reminder that nothing is static in the natural world.

—— IN ——

February

If Candlemas Day be bright an' fair
Half o' da winter's tae come and mair
But if Candlemas Day be dark an' dull
Half o' da winter wis dune at Yule

Candlemas Day is the 2nd of February and the Shetland version of this well-known saying indicates the importance of this date in predicting future weather. Folklore emphasises that a mild February is a portent of further severe wintry conditions before spring establishes itself. February comes from the Latin *februa* a means of purification, referring to an ancient Roman ceremony held at this time of year. In Shetland it is one of the coldest months with bitter winds being drawn down across the islands from the Arctic. High rainfall is also a feature, with lochs and burns overflowing, although the latter part of the month is often drier enabling spring ploughing to get under way in some parts of the islands.

Shags and cormorants are collecting pieces of seaweed and vegetation to repair their untidy sprawling nests in readiness for egg laying in April. Shags typically nest at the base of cliffs, on stacks and inside sea caves. At close quarters the adult plumage is a dark bottle-green shot with purple tints. The eyes are vivid emerald and there is a yellow gape patch at the base of the bill. Exclusively marine, their main diet is mid-water fish such as sand eels, whiting and, especially, juvenile *saithe*. Widespread and resident throughout the islands, the breeding population numbers several thousand pairs.

Cormorants are also widely distributed but most of the breeding colonies are confined to the North and West Mainland with a total population of just over 500 birds. Nests are generally sited on flat-topped sea stacks, cliff edges and small islands. Larger thicker-necked, and with a heavier bill than the shag, adult cormorants have dark blue-black plumage with a bronze sheen on the upperparts. During the breeding season they develop conspicuous white patches on the thighs, cheeks and throat. Cormorants also catch fish but, in addition to marine species, they also take trout and eels from freshwater lochs.

Both cormorants and shags swim low in the water and can slowly submerge their bodies leaving only the head and neck visible. When diving, air is first expelled from the feathers to increase overall density, before a plunging leap is made from the surface. The prey is usually eaten at the surface, the bird first adroitly juggling the fish into a head-first position for swallowing. Cormorants and shags are often seen standing around with outstretched wings like heraldic emblems. Lacking the oily water-repellent coating which protects the feathers of other seabirds, prolonged immersion results in their feathers becoming water-logged and requiring drying. This outstretched wing posture also aids digestion of the fish.

They share the cold slate-grey seas with wintering sea duck. Alongside the flocks of eider and long-tailed duck, small numbers of common scoter and occasional velvet scoter occur. Scoters are usually recorded in shallow waters offshore where they dive frequently feeding on invertebrates and small fish. Slightly larger than long tails, male common scoters are jet black except for some yellow on the bill. The females are sooty brown with conspicuous white cheeks. A few pairs of this species breed in Shetland but the main breeding grounds are further north.

Velvet scoters are almost the size of an eider and have heavy-looking heads and thick bills. The male is glossy black with a small white crescent-shaped mark behind the eye and yellow bordering on the dark bill, although first year males are browner. The female is dark brown with some greyish barring on the upperparts and has two small pale head patches. Both sexes display a white wingbar in flight. Velvet scoters have a holarctic breeding distribution.

On freshwater lochs throughout the islands wintering duck populations are decreasing as many start heading north to breed in Scandinavia, Russia, Iceland and Greenland. During February, reasonable numbers of tufted duck, goldeneye and mallard still remain with small flocks of pochards on some lochs. Male tufted duck, black and white with a drooping crest and bright yellow eye, are accompanied by the

Tufted Duck

duller females. Male goldeneyes, also in striking black and white plumage, court their mates extending and throwing back their heads in display. Wintering mallards are already paired up which enable them to start breeding as soon as they return to their northerly breeding grounds.

Coots and moorhens occur mainly as passage migrants and winter visitors although small numbers of moorhens breed in Shetland. Both species are easily distinguished at a distance from ducks by their dumpy shape, pointed bills and smaller size. Moorhens swim with a characteristic jerky motion, raising the tail out of the water and constantly bobbing the head and neck. They rarely dive and usually feed close to the shore or on damp marshy land taking a variety of plants and invertebrates. At close quarters, the moorhen's plumage of olive-brown back, slate-grey underparts with white-streaked flanks and deep red forehead and bill is diagnostic. The coot has a striking white bill and forehead which contrasts with the smoky-grey plumage. They prefer open water, swimming with the tail low on the water, neck hunched, and small head moving back and fore. Coots make frequent short dives feeding on submerged water plants and aquatic invertebrates.

Fields and rough pasture provide important winter feeding grounds for flocks of waders. Birds in flocks improve their feeding efficiency as greater numbers increase the chance of finding good food supplies and individuals benefit from the experience of other members of the flock. Flocking also has an anti-predatory function – approaching danger is more likely to be detected by many eyes than by a solitary bird.

Small flocks of lapwings remain in the islands but many will move further south during very cold spells. This species is particularly sensitive to the increasing cold as their food supply becomes locked up in impenetrable frosty earth. Feeding lapwings spread out over a field, foraging in typical plover fashion. A bird runs a short distance, stops, peers at the ground then bends forwards and pecks at suitable prey. The bulk of their diet consists of earthworms, insects and insect larvae which are caught on or just below the surface of the soil.

Around the second week of February ringed plovers, the majority of which winter outwith Shetland, return to their breeding sites. Flocks of turnstones feed in arable fields at high tide. They are usually seen in small flocks of about twenty, quartering the ground in tight ever-moving groups but on large re-seeded fields over a hundred may gather. These turnstones are mainly winter and passage migrants, several thousand spending the winter in Shetland before returning to the Arctic to breed. The flocks are frequently accompanied by small numbers of redshanks. Easily recognised by its red legs and bill, the redshank displays a broad white trailing edge to the wing in flight and a distinctive white rump extending up the back between the wings. The flight is fast and rather erratic with sudden changes of direction.

Stately groups of curlew also probe the winter fields and shoreline, their long, down-curved bills capable of reaching up to 15cm/6ins below the surface. Large flocks of golden plover, banking alternately golden and white, flight in to feed on grassy fields. On the ground their characteristic upright stance identifies them even at a distance. By February they are acquiring the beautiful golden-spangled upperparts contrasting with smart black 'shirt fronts' of their breeding plumage. By the end of the month oystercatchers are returning in numbers, their familiar resonant 'kleep' calls providing a welcome reminder of spring.

Starlings are also preparing for the breeding season. On calm days males begin to sing from prominent perches, puffing out their glossy throat feathers and displaying their iridescent feathers. During the winter months their bills are a dull brown but, by February, increasing hormonal activity produces a colour change to yellow, the colour flooding gradually down the bill from base to tip. Bill colour also starts to differentiate the sexes as the base of the male's bill turns light blue whilst that of the female becomes pinkish. The legs and feet of breeding starlings also change from brown to reddish pink.

A few species of small garden birds usually overwinter. Sheltered gardens with trees and shrubs may harbour finches such as greenfinch and chaffinch or even an occasional bullfinch or great tit.

Fields and pasture attract species such as redwing, fieldfare and snow bunting or *snaa fool*. Male snow buntings in breeding plumage are boldly patterned in black and

Snow Bunting

28

white, whilst females are speckled brown and black on the upperparts with snowy white underparts. Their stocky, rounded bodies combined with dense plumage helps them combat extreme cold. The long broad wings are designed for efficient control in high winds, the strong, undulating flight giving the impression of the flock swirling into the air like snowflakes on take off. Wintering snow buntings are often seen in agricultural areas where they glean any left over seeds or take advantage of livestock feeding sites.

Common seals favour sheltered voes and bays earning them their Shetland name of *tangfish* - 'tang' being the brown kelps which grow in shallow waters. Smaller than our other native species, the grey seal, common seals measure about 1.75m/5.75ft and weigh 80-100kg/176-220lb. Other distinguishing features are the V-shaped nostrils, rounded dog-like head and spotty coat pattern. Colours range from dark steely grey to the palest biscuit but the coat is generally covered in smaller darker spots than the larger blotches of the grey seal.

They often haul out and remain ashore for several hours, occasionally waving a foreflipper or lazily flicking their tails. Common seals also take advantage of the sheltered conditions created by the construction of small boat marinas around the Shetland coastline. Sometimes they adopt a typical U-shaped stance with the head and tail raised high or just slump on the rocks like large furry slugs. Their habits are largely governed by the tidal cycle. Feeding at high tide, they return shorewards as the tide ebbs. Common seals, unlike greys, have complex cusped teeth which enable them to consume a wide variety of prey including shellfish, crustaea and squid as well as fish such as herring, mackerel, skate, cod and sandeels.

At this time of year sea temperatures are at their lowest and rocky seashores appear rather lifeless as many of inter-tidal organisms have moved out into deeper water during the winter months. However, as the spring plankton blooms slowly begin to get under way, some marine organisms are starting to reproduce. Acorn barnacles, cemented securely to the rocks throughout the winter storms, now release larvae into the plankton.

Acorn Barnacles

Having mated in the autumn, the liberation of the floating larvae is timed to coincide with a period of abundant food in the upper layers of the sea so that by April/May the juvenile barnacles are settling out on rocks in the inter-tidal zones of seashores. At the same time juvenile brown and white sea slugs, *Onchidoris bimellata* are beginning to appear inshore to feast off the bonanza of colonising barnacle spat. This species feeds almost exclusively on acorn barnacles so that its breeding cycle is closely timetabled to that of the barnacles. During February thousands of larval *Onchidoris* are joining their future prey in the plankton.

Plant life is still at a low ebb so any green growth is conspicuous. Brightening up burns and ditches are the lime-green masses of common water starwort, *Callitriche stagnalis,* its straggly branching thread-like stems giving this

29

plant its genus name meaning 'beautiful hair' in Greek. The delicate stems bear opposite pairs of oval-shaped leaves which appear to form a star shape when seen from above. Small rootlets growing from the stem sides attach the plant loosely to the muddy bottom although it can also float free. It provides an important source of oxygen for the animal life found in stagnant or slow-moving waters.

Also growing on stones in the same habitat is a distinctive water moss, *Fontinalis antipyretica,* or willow moss. The leaves are borne in three ranks along elongated, branching stems and remain green throughout the winter providing shelter for small, aquatic invertebrates. The specific name *antipyretica* means 'against fire' and refers to the use of willow moss as a non-inflammable insulating material in the walls of wooden houses in Lapland.

On the moorland, the dull browns and ochres of heather and dead grasses are enlivened by colourful cushions of mosses. The most conspicuous are species of *Sphagnum* moss which range in colour from vivid emerald through bright yellow-greens, to palest lemons, subtle beiges and ethereal pinks to rich wine-reds. These mosses are ingenuously designed to retain water. The tiny overlapping leaves help to trap moisture, the branches at the tip typically forming a tight head whilst the lower branches grow vertically. This design helps to wick the water downwards into the spongy carpet of tightly-packed moss stems. Within the leaves are specialised water-retaining cells which form a con-tinuous interconnecting network throughout the leaf. Water is held in these cells thus creating a squishy water-logged cushion or hummock.

Sphagnum Moss

The first spring bulbs appear this month such as snowdrops, early crocus and winter aconite. By the end of February winter's grip is lessening and more signs of spring begin to appear.

─── IN ───
March

March ....Comes in like a lion
Goes out like a lamb.

March takes its name from Mars, the Roman god of war. There is frequently more of the 'lion' than the 'lamb' in March weather in Shetland. It is officially the first month of spring but the weather often oscillates between the seasons with cold blustery gales and calm mild intervals. This variability may make spring a slow stop-start process. Increasing daylength triggers reproduction in animals and plants but cool temperatures and unfavourable weather conditions can delay further development. At the equinox, around the 21st of the month, the hours of daylength equal those of darkness as the northern hemisphere inexorably tilts towards the sun again.

Seabirds, which have spent the winter at sea, head towards their breeding grounds this month. Guillemots and razorbills move inshore, forming large floating rafts below the breeding cliffs prior to re-colonising the nesting ledges. By the end of March the first puffins are returning looking plump and newly-refurbished,

Eiders

31

although they will not take up full residence until next month. Kittiwakes also return from their pelagic wanderings in the North Atlantic and North Sea, their familiar, onomatopoeic calls echoing amongst the cliff faces. The nests are built on the narrowest of ledges and are constructed from green seaweed, grasses, moss and other vegetation all cemented together by guano. Kittiwakes are one of six gull species which breed in Shetland – the others being great back-backed gull, herring gull, lesser black-backed gull, common gull and black-headed gull.

Battalions of gannets are arriving at the large breeding colonies of Noss and Hermaness – smaller numbers breed on Foula and Fair Isle. Gannets are the largest of the British seabirds and are recognisable, even at considerable distances, by their white plumage, black-tipped wings and sea-skimming flight. Throughout the winter months the pairs separate, reuniting at the breeding colonies in the spring. Gannets are long-lived seabirds which generally pair for life and now these pair-bonds are reinforced by noisy ritualised displays.

Inshore, black guillemots or *tysties* are moulting out of their grey and white winter plumage into a sleek summer dress of glossy black with contrasting white wing patches. These auks remain around the Shetland coastline throughout the year feeding on small inshore fish such as butterfish and rockling supplemented by crustaceans and molluscs. In spring they form loose flocks and take part in communal displays before the breeding season begins. Their call is a rather plaintive, shrill whistle. Adding to this spring chorus are the surprised-sounding 'oos' of courting eider ducks. The males, resplendent in their black and white breeding plumage with green nape patches and pink-tinged breasts, throw back their heads in noisy display to attract the less conspicuous brown females. Eiders are resident throughout the year with an estimated present population of about 7,000. They feed mainly on mussels and crabs caught inshore.

Ravens, the largest of the crow family, nest in March with eggs appearing by the end of the month. In flight the large size, wedge-shaped tail and upturned primary feathers are diagnostic features. During courtship they perform amazing aerial displays of somersaulting, tumbling and diving. One bird may suddenly flip on to its back in flight, close its wings and drop a few feet before resuming normal flight. The nest is a large structure, used year after year and constructed from materials such as twigs, seaweed, heather stems and bones, lined with earth and sheep's wool. Most are built on sea cliffs although some inland sites are also used.

The hooded crow, the northern race of the carrion crow, is also resident in Shetland. Hooded crows are found north and west of an approximate line drawn along the Caledonian Canal, with the all-black carrion crow occurring south of this line. Hybrids between the two races occur in areas of overlap. In Shetland hoodies are widespread and common. Being extremely opportunistic feeders they have a varied diet ranging from earthworms to rabbits. Nest sites are generally on sea cliffs, in trees or on

Rook

32

heather moorland.

Rooks also start breeding this month. The only rookery in the islands is at Kergord where the untidy twiggy nests are built in the tops of a clump of mature trees. Adult rooks are easily identified by the bare whitish facial patch and loose thigh feathers, giving the bird the appearance of wearing 'baggy trousers'. Around Kergord and in areas such as Tingwall and Nesting, rooks can often be seen foraging in the fields. They are specialised grassland feeders, probing the ground with highly sensitive bills in their search for worms, leather jackets and other invertebrates. The species is also recorded as a passage migrant and winter visitor, a few birds generally being recorded in other parts of Shetland during spring and autumn.

Skylarks and meadow pipits start to return towards the end of the month. Starlings, glossy and iridescent in their breeding plumage, sing loudly from stone walls and fence posts. As the month progresses, oystercatcher flocks break up into individual pairs. Lapwings begin displaying over their breeding territories, calling loudly and tumbling through the air in a flurry of piebald feathers. After dusk, the quivering calls of drumming snipe may be heard. The sound is produced by vibrating air passing over the outer tail feathers. Displaying males also have a loud 'chip-pa' call. The first migrants are usually recorded in March, often small warblers such as chiffchaffs.

On freshwater lochs many of the wildfowl winter visitors will have departed for their breeding grounds further north. Resident mallards are already seeking out suitable nesting sites in long waterside vegetation. By now many of Shetland's breeding red-throated divers have returned and are elegantly patrolling their watery territories. Around 420 pairs breed in

Red-throated Diver

the islands, the majority nesting on the shores of peaty lochs on blanket bog. The red throat is only clearly visible in bright light but the slightly upturned bill readily identifies this species. The Shetland name is *raingoose* from the loud quacking calls made as the diver flies from the moorland lochs down to the sea to feed. The direction of travel was supposed to foretell the weather whilst the call is likened to 'weet ower 'aa'. Red-throated divers also utter loud eerie wailing calls when displaying.

Mammals are also feeling the stirrings of spring. Most adult female rabbits are pregnant by now, having mated earlier in the year. Dominant does give birth in the main warren but subordinate females have to leave and establish shallow nursing burrows elsewhere. Young females give birth to four young but the average litter size is six. Whilst the female is suckling she is already pregnant with the next litter, producing an average of twelve young per year. The young are independent at about a month old.

Increasing daylight and warmer temperatures trigger the moult in mountain hares. Their patchy white and brown fur is exchanged for a grey-brown summer coat with paler flanks and greyish-white underparts. At this time of year the males chase and spar with the females, the two animals rearing up on their hind legs and boxing each other with their forepaws. As the female hare comes into season she releases a pheromone which excites the males but she will not allow him near until she is fully receptive.

During March mature common frogs return to ponds and ditches to spawn. Waking from hibernation, the males arrive first and croak loudly to attract females. In preparation for the breeding season they grow spiny pads on the thumbs of their forefeet which are used for clasping the slippery body of the female. The appearance of a female provokes a rugby scrum-like mass of jostling males, each trying to be the first to clasp her in a tight piggy-back embrace. The successful suitor remains firmly clamped to the female for hours, even days, until she sheds her eggs. As the eggs appear he releases a cloud of sperm and the pair then separate leaving the fertilised eggs to sink to the bottom of the pond. However, contact with the water causes the jelly-like protective layer to swell up and the eggs rise to the surface forming the familiar gelatinous mass of frog spawn.

Common Frog

Down on the seashore other animals are also spawning. Lumpsuckers are stout-bodied fish with sticky lumpy skin and four rows of bony spines protruding along each side. On the underside is a powerful pelvic sucker which attaches the fish to rocks. In early spring lumpsuckers come close inshore to spawn, after which the female returns to deeper water. The male, however, remains to guard and aerate the egg masses until they hatch in about 5-6 weeks. During the breeding season the male develops a brilliant reddish-orange belly and flanks and can sometimes be found at extremely low spring tides.

Lumpsucker

These low tides, caused by the March equinox, provide good opportunities to explore the lowest regions of the shore which are normally submerged. The greatest variety of organisms will be found on sheltered rocky shores. Amongst the kelp tangles sessile organisms such as sponges, dahlia sea anemones, hydroids, bryozoans and sea squirts can be found. Beneath the seaweed and rocks may be small fish such as rocklings and butterfish, or polychaete worms. There may also be starfish, brittlestars and sea urchins and, in addition to shore crabs, small specimens of edible crabs or the triangular seaweed-festooned carapace of a spider crab. Sea slugs, such as the common grey sea slug and the sea lemon, also reproduce in spring.

A close examination of kelp fronds may also reveal kingfisher or blue-rayed limpets, *Patina pellucida pellucidum*. These tiny molluscs grow up to a maximum length of 2cm/¾ins and have smooth golden-brown translucent shells with lines of bright blue spots arching down from the apex. The other sub-species, *laevis*, lives

34

inside the kelp holdfast where they eat out deep rounded cavities. The activity of the kingfisher limpet can so weaken the holdfast that the kelp stem snaps off in winter storms. Few kelp plants survive for longer than eight years.

A calm sunny day may bring out hibernating insects, activated by an increase in temperature. One of the first is often the notorious bluebottle which spends the winter tucked into sheltered crevices. Bluebottles which enter houses are usually females searching for somewhere to lay their eggs. Small overwintering moths, such as the white-shouldered house moth, may also make their re-appearance indoors this month.

March also brings the first flowers of spring. Snowdrops and early crocus are followed by the cheering yellows of daffodils and narcissi and then the more varied hues of tulips and other spring bulbs. One of the earliest of the wildflowers to appear is the coltsfoot. It is a colonist in Shetland, i.e., an accidental introduction, and occurs around crofts and farms, on weedy roadside banks, rubble heaps and alongside burns. The golden yellow flower heads are borne on long stems studded with pinkish scales which help to insulate the developing plant from the cold. After flowering the flower heads bend over to protect the maturing seeds which are dispersed by fluffy parachutes. The large leaves, which give the plant its common name, only appear after the plant has flowered and set its seeds.

Coltsfoot

Another early-flowering species is lesser celandine, a native of the islands, which is usually found in damp shady areas, often beneath trees. The glossy rather fragile-looking yellow petals often fade to white as the plant matures. The buttercup-like flower heads rise from clumps of long-stalked heart-shaped leaves.

Tussi-girse also flowers at this time of year. This coarse tussock-forming grass was introduced to Shetland from islands in the sub-Antarctic. It is mainly found growing near crofts in the South Mainland but is also recorded from Bousta in Sandness and grows at Ham in Bressay. It is widely believed that tussock grass was brought to Shetland by islanders employed in the whaling at South Georgia, or in sheep farming in the Falkland Islands. However, it is known that there were attempts to grow this plant from seed during the nineteenth century. The tussock grass at Fladdabister has been there since at least 1900 and that on Bressay since the 1880s.

In spring willows produce catkins which develop along the twigs before the leaves emerge. Each tree is either male or female and both bear nectar-producing catkins, fertilisation being achieved by early-flying insects. Several native, introduced and hybrid species of willow occur in Shetland, often planted around crofts and in gardens. Willows have the advantage of growing in both peaty and mineral soils, thriving in wet conditions and growing well from cuttings. The winter buds of willows can be recognised as each leaf is enclosed in a single scale like a covering cap.

By the end of March buds on trees and bushes are swelling and some brave specimens, such as honeysuckle and flowering currant, are tentatively unfurling their leaves whilst the first wild flowers start to brighten up the landscape.

Bell heather, Voehead Road, Bressay.

Wild flowers, Unst.

Mimulus, Sandwick.

Red campion.

Puffins, Hermaness.

Gannet colony, Hermaness.

Common seal pup.

Sunset, Lunna.

——— IN ———
April

The uncertain glory of an April day
Which now shows all the beauty of the sun,
And by and by a cloud takes all away.

William Shakespeare

A pril is a month of contrasts. As spring struggles to assert itself the weather is
often subject to sudden reversions to cold blustery conditions. 'April' comes
from a Latin word meaning 'opening' as leaves and flowers unfold. However, the
word traditionally associated with this month is 'showers', a weather condition
which can often be an understatement at his time of year in Shetland when the
islands are still under the influence of the vagaries of depressions sweeping in from
the North Atlantic.

As the ground starts to dry up the soil temperatures rise, and 'voar work' can
take place on crofts and farms. Spring sowing gets under way and, when soil
temperatures increase to 5°C, plant growth is stimulated. Lambing begins in the
more southerly parts of the islands such as Fair Isle and the South Mainland, the
newly-born lambs initially staying close to their mothers. Daylight hours are
lengthening appreciably. At the beginning of April the sun rises at around 6.30am
and sets at about 7.50pm British Summertime.

Near the base of the seabird cliffs shags are already brooding clutches of
three pale blue eggs in their large untidy nests. Kittiwakes visit freshwater lochs to
bathe and to collect mud to repair their nests. Gannets are also involved in nest
re-construction. The other cliff tenants – fulmars, herring and black-backed gulls –
are already well established by the time the auks return. Returning guillemots stake
their claim to a section of narrow ledge whilst crevice-nesting razorbills threaten
intruders with sharp white-chevroned bills. The first puffins gather in huge rafts
below their colonies before taking to the air in a 'wheel' – a circular flightpath,
which alternately passes over the burrows on the cliffs and then flies out over the
sea. Gradually a few birds leave the whirling mass of the fly-past and touch down
near their burrows.

Puffins do not usually come ashore until they are about two or three years
old and do not attain full breeding status until they are about five. They can be aged
by the appearance of their beaks. The colourful beak sheath is grown anew each
spring and shed in the autumn, as are the other facial ornaments which give the bird
its appealing character. As the puffin matures the beak sheaths become larger, the
colours intensify and more grooves appear on the red part. When a puffin is under
two years old it is difficult to see any beak grooves and the bill is relatively smaller

and less bulky than that of an older bird. At three years old there is at least one groove visible and, by four, two beak grooves are present. Some puffins acquire an additional groove in later years.

Breeding adults arrive first at the colonies, each pair returning to the same burrow used last year. Favoured burrow sites are sloping cliff tops with soft soil which the birds can dig into, but they also nest amongst boulders and scree. Puffins need to nest in places from which they can quickly become airborne. Most breeding birds retain the same mate each year, re-uniting at the nest burrow after wintering in the North Atlantic. The pair bond is re-established by digging out old nest material and refurbishing the burrows, and by billing – clattering their beaks together.

During April skuas are returning to breed on moorlands throughout Shetland. First to arrive are the great skuas or *bonxies,* their bulky thick-set appearance matching their piratical and murderous behaviour towards other species of seabirds. Looking like large brown-streaked gulls with white wing patches, they utter a querulous 'uuk uuk' call as they fly overhead. The nest is merely a scrape in the heather, sometimes lined with dead grasses, but the territory around the site is ferociously defended against all intruders. The Shetland population is estimated at around 6,200 breeding pairs which is almost half the world bonxie population.

Arctic skuas arrive back later, usually after mid-April. They prefer drier habitats than bonxies with shorter vegetation. Smaller and slimmer than bonxies, Arctics have elongated central tail feathers which project beyond the end of the tail. The plumage is variable with light, dark and intermediate colour phases. They are also fiercely territorial and swoop fearlessly at anything entering their territory. The breeding population of around 1,900 is less than a third of that of the bonxies and makes up about 61% of the British Arctic skua population.

Shetland moorlands are particularly important for breeding birds. By now breeding waders have established territories, the mournful call of the golden plover being a characteristic sound of many tracts of moorland. The winter flocks of curlew have dispersed and their haunting calls echo over rough pasture and heather moorland as they prepare for the breeding season.

Arctic Skua

From mid-April onwards whimbrel return from their winter quarters in Africa. The breeding population of over 400 pairs, about 95% of the British total, is mainly concentrated on the islands of Unst and Fetlar. Some pairs breed on the Mainland and, during April, migrating whimbrel are commonly seen, or more often, heard throughout the islands. The whimbrel has a very distinctive tittering seven note whistle, often uttered as the bird is flying overhead. Whimbrel can also be distinguished from curlew by their smaller size, faster wing beats, shorter bill and striped pattern on the crown of the head.

Another summer visitor is also returning from Africa. The wheatear or *steynshakker* announces its arrival by its hard 'chack chack' call, sounding like two stones being struck together – hence its Shetland name. The common name comes from an Anglo Saxon word meaning 'white rump'. The wheatear constantly bobs up and down, flicking its wings and wagging its tail showing off the white rump against the black inverted T of the tail tip. Breeding wheatears can be found throughout Shetland, favouring rough pastures, rocky moorland and roadsides. In spring larger more brightly coloured birds, belonging to the Greenland race, are commonly seen on passage.

Wheatear

April usually brings the first 'fall' of spring migrants. The largest falls occur when south east winds are accompanied by an advancing front of foggy or rainy weather. Birds on their way north to breed in Scandinavia and beyond, can no longer navigate and are forced to land. Exhausted migrants seek out areas with cover such as clumps of trees or shrubs but, in Shetland, they can turn up anywhere such as in cropped and grassy fields, geos, vegetated slopes on sea cliffs and sheltering in the lee of stone dykes. Males are in breeding plumage in spring which makes identification easier. The first migrants are often chiffchaffs, robins, dunnocks, goldcrests, song thrushes and blackbirds, sometimes accompanied by fieldfares and redwings. As the month progresses other regular migrants such as chaffinch, brambling, pied wagtail, blackcap, willow warbler, redstart, sand martin and swallow may be recorded.

Migrants can occur anywhere in Shetland but are most often recorded from the east coast, the South Mainland and Fair Isle. The world-famous Fair Isle bird observatory has recorded vagrants from as far away as North America and Asia. It is wonderful to experience a good fall on Fair Isle when the entire island becomes a huge stepping stone for thousands of disorientated and hungry migrants. One particular day the approaching front brought with it a fine mist from which materialised ghostly forms. Most numerous were large flocks of fieldfares which landed in fields in the south part of the island. At rest these long-winged, long-tailed birds frequently droop their wings, producing a very characteristic silhouette even in poor light conditions. Interspersed amongst the fieldfares, roughly on a ratio of one to five, were redwings with their distinctive upright stance and rusty-red flanks. Robins appeared to be everywhere, reddish breasts glowing, as they hopped along the drystane dykes, flitted around the steep-sided geos and fluttered amongst the dead grasses beside the road. Common redstarts accompanied them, their tails like orange flames. Tiny goldcrests called as they hunted amongst tufts of vegetation on the seacliffs, their high-pitched notes rising above the clamour of the sea. A male blackcap paused on a rocky boulder, looking incongruous against a background of pounding fleecy surf. Flocks of finches fed around the stackyards and sheep feeding troughs. Brambling rose and re-settled like black and orange confetti blown in the wind. Colourful chaffinches were joined by the monochrome beauty of three male snow buntings. Other migrants which arrived that day included blackbird, song thrush, dunnock, Greenland wheatear, chiffchaff and a great grey shrike. The latter did me the courtesy of sitting quite unperturbed on a stone wall allowing excellent views.

Mammals are into their breeding season by April. Male hedgehogs which emerged last month need to replenish their reserves. During hibernation the males' reproductive organs shrink as fat deposits are consumed and the animal loses up to one third of its body weight. However, within a month of emergence, the males have put on weight, come into breeding condition and begin to travel widely in search of a mate. As the first young rabbits of the year are beginning to scamper around the fields, providing ready prey for predators, small mammals such as mice and rats are also starting to breed.

Otters generally breed at any time of year but in Shetland mating activity occurs in the spring to ensure that cubs are born during summer when food is plentiful. Shetland's otter population, estimated at 850-1,100, is of international importance, the islands being one of the main strongholds for otters in Britain. Originally adapted to life in freshwater rivers, the Shetland otters are virtually marine animals, living and feeding along the coastline. However an essential prerequisite is the presence of freshwater within their area in which they can wash the salt water from their pelts. Otters have no thick layer of blubber like seals and rely on the insulating properties of their fur to protect them from the cold northern waters. For much of the year they are solitary animals except when a female is rearing cubs or during the spring mating season. At this time of year dog otters, whose ranges overlap those of several groups of females, go in search of a mate. Both sexes may mate with more than one partner, the females being left alone to rear the cubs. Favourite otter habitats are low rocky shores backed by peaty hillside through which flow one or more freshwater burns.

Along the rocky shores seaweed cover is increasing including the filamentous green seaweeds such as *Enteromorpha*, *Ulva* and *Cladophora*. *Cladophora rupestris* grows in dense dark green wiry tufts around the mid-shore. The commonest species of green seaweed is *Enteromorpha intestinalis*, also known as gutweed, which grows on the upper shore in thick pale green bubbly masses. *Ulva lactuca* or sea lettuce grows mid-shore in small bunches of broad membranous wavy fronds.

Warmer temperatures encourage the appearance of flying insects. Flies and midges are on the wing on milder days. Towards the end of April the first white-tailed bumblebees emerge from hibernation. These are females which fly in a zigzag fashion above the ground searching for a suitable hole in which to make a nest and found a new colony. Another early insect is the Hebrew character moth. The reddish-grey forewings are embellished with distinctive dark markings resembling the letter C. These moths visit sallow

White-tailed Bumblebee

40

catkins at dusk and are attracted to lighted windows.

Throughout April more plants come into flower, the exact dates depending on weather and temperatures. Many of the first spring flowers are yellow - a colour which attracts early-flying insects. Primroses are native to Shetland growing in calcareous soils on cliffs, grassy coastal slopes, fields, along burns and on roadside banks. Another spring flower is the pale blue spring squill which spangles cliff tops and grassy areas and, in places, contrasts with rose pink clumps of moss campion.

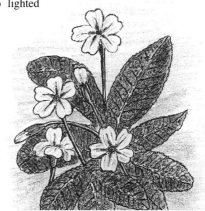

Primrose

Moss campion is a hardy Arctic-alpine, found above 600m/1,968ft elsewhere, which occurs in Shetland at sea level due to the effect of latitude on altitude. It grows as a compact dense cushion, characteristic features for lessening wind resistance and susceptibility to water loss. In early spring the cushions are spray-scoured and brown but gradually, tiny pin-points of green emerge until the clump is transformed into a lush moss-like mass of tiny leaves. The tightly furled red buds emerge to stipple the surface before opening to reveal the delicate blush-pink five-petalled flowers.

Soon, as the year moves into May, burnished golden swags of marsh marigolds transform wet areas and the delicate lilac flowers of lady's smock appear in damp pastures heralding the summer riot of colour in these flower-rich areas.

— IN —
May

Rough winds do shake the darling buds of May
And summer's lease hath all too short a date.

William Shakespeare

In Shetland rough, and sometimes bitterly cold, winds can do a lot more damage than shaking May buds. A wintry gale can shrivel up the new leaves and strip the twigs bare. However the latter part of the month usually brings more settled weather and rainfall decreases. Lambing occurs throughout much of the islands coinciding with the growth of fresh green pasture. Crofters are also busy with spring cultivation and peat cutting. Gardeners burst into activity, remedying winter ravages and planning out the season's planting. By mid-May hours of daylight have increased to around seventeen and the nights of the 'simmer dim' are with us again.

The seabird cliffs resonate with noise and activity as courtship, egg laying and incubation progress. Most of the large seabird colonies occur on cliffs composed of sedimentary rock. The commonest type, Old Red Sandstone, formed 350-400 million years ago, forms the basis for the colonies at Noss, Sumburgh Head, Fair Isle and Foula. Sedimentary rock forms from layers of sediment which settle out under water. The deepest layers are subjected to considerable pressure which squeezes out the water and consolidates the particles into rock. Sedimentary rocks have distinct layering or *stratification* caused by slight changes in the composition of the layers as they were laid down. The layers weather unevenly to produce a series of ledges and crevices which can be used by breeding seabirds. However, not every sandstone cliff provides suitable nesting habitat. Various factors such as height above sea level, degrees of stratification of the rock and the angle of strata all affect the suitability. An ideal seabird cliff has almost horizontal strata with many bedding planes which have eroded unevenly – the best example in Shetland being the cliffs on the island of Noss.

Different seabird species have different strategies for ensuring successful incubation of their eggs. Nest-building species such as gulls develop small featherless patches on their breasts, known as 'brood patches'. These areas are richly supplied with blood and provide neat-fitting pockets in which the eggs nestle snugly when the bird is incubating. Gannets build large untidy nests but they are not equipped with brood patches. Instead, they use their large webbed feet to provide the egg with warmth and protection. Guillemots lay their eggs on the bare ledges and, unlike most other species, actually recognise their own egg by its markings. The eggs are pear-shaped so that, if moved, they spin round in a circle rather than over the edge into the sea. Burrow-nesters such as puffins lay plain light-coloured eggs which gleam in the dim light filtering in from the burrow entrance.

The length of incubation in seabirds depends mainly on the size of the egg in relation to its yolk content. The more yolk present, the more reserves will be available for the newly-hatched chick. Seabirds belonging to the petrel family, such as fulmars and storm petrels, have long incubation periods. The tiny stormie incubates its egg for almost forty one days. This is an adaptation to the food supply provided by the parents. Petrels feed on plankton and other animal matter floating on the surface of the sea and are frequently away from the nest site for long intervals. The newly-hatched petrel chicks are provided with ample food reserves to give them a good start whilst the parents are away foraging.

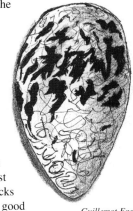

Guillemot Egg

In early May the bird, which is often thought of as the true harbinger of spring in Shetland, arrives – the Arctic tern or *tirrick*. Arctic terns enjoy more hours of daylight than any other birds by breeding in the northern hemisphere and wintering in the southern hemisphere. Ringing recoveries have shown that most of our breeding Arctic terns winter off the coast of West Africa. These terns can be distinguished from common terns by their longer tail streamers and blood-red bills. The flight is also more buoyant and the call note is harsher. Common terns, which also breed in Shetland but in far fewer numbers, have scarlet bills with a contrasting black tip.

Over the last fifteen years Shetland Arctic tern populations have decreased drastically – by a factor of over 50% since 1980. The cause appears to be a combination of cold summers and food shortages. The main component of their diet are sand eels which are caught by shallow plunge diving. Research during the late 1980s showed that Arctic terns were unable to supply their chicks with suitably-sized sand eels resulting in widespread and dramatic breeding failure throughout the islands.

Terns nest colonially on shingly beaches and coastal vegetation, defending the site fiercely against intruders. The aerial bombardment is accompanied by loud screaming 'kee yah' calls. Colonies are subject to fluctuations from year to year, sites which have been used for several years suddenly being abandoned. Tern couples usually pair for life and the male re-establishes the pair bond by bringing the female courtship presents of fish. The speckled eggs are laid in a simple scrape and incubated for about a month.

Redshanks are also incubating by the middle of May. The adults spring from grassy fields and damp hay meadows, their loud cries sharp with anxiety. The nest is usually built in the centre of a large tussock of grass or sedge. Nesting redshanks are indicative of the potential of an area to support other common breeding waders. If an area of marshy habitat has two or three pairs of nesting redshank then it will also support species such as breeding curlew and snipe. Redshank lay four eggs and incubation lasts for about three weeks.

Over grassland and rough pasture skylarks and meadow pipits are displaying. Male skylarks sing to advertise the fact that the territory is occupied, each display flight lasting for about five minutes. The lark flies jerkily upwards, circling until it is a tiny pulsing sound-source high above. Singing males stimulate others so that the whole sky appears to reverberate with lark song. The flight ends dramatically as the bird folds its wings and plunges downward, fluttering its wings open again just before landing. Meadow pipits also have a characteristic song flight consisting of a sequence of short notes as the bird flies upwards followed by a descending trill as the bird parachutes to the ground.

During May the spring migration continues with species such as garden warbler, sedge warbler cuckoo, redstart, whinchat, whitethroat, lesser whitethroat, pied and spotted flycatchers, red-backed shrike, bluethroat, sand martin, swallow and house martin regularly occurring in the islands. The red-backed shrike is a classic spring migrant. The male is a particularly handsome bird with reddish-brown wings and back, white underparts, grey crown and rump, and black mask and tail. Shrikes have powerful-looking hooked bills, feeding on large insects and small birds which they sometimes impale on sharp points to form a larder for future use.

Swallow

Male bluethroats are also striking migrants. Superficially resembling a robin in size, build and behaviour the adult male lives up to its name with a brilliant azure-blue gorget edged by bands of first black and then chestnut feathers. In the midst of the blue throat area there is either a red or white spot, depending on which race the bird belongs to. Red-spotted forms are the commonest recorded in Shetland, breeding in Scandinavia and Russia. The female is duller having a black ring of throat feathers with traces of chestnut. Both sexes have a distinctive white eyestripe and rufous patches at the base of the tail.

More commonly seen spring migrants are swallows and house martins. A few pairs of swallows generally breed at widespread locations throughout the islands but most are migrants on route to Scandinavia. They are most frequently seen hawking insects, often over water, to provide fuel for the next stage of the journey. Swallows are easily recognised by their burnished blue-black upperparts, paler underparts, red chins and deeply-forked tails. They characteristically fly low, skimming the ground, in fast twisting flight. About 80% of the prey consists of flies, and areas with cow pats provide good hunting grounds. The house martin is a smaller, shorter-winged bird with a conspicuous white rump contrasting with the brownish wings and tail and blue-black back. The flight is less aerobatic than that of the swallow, and the species breeds occasionally in Shetland.

Mammals are well into their breeding season by now. Young bunnies are everywhere but many will not survive to maturity as they run a gauntlet of cats, dogs, polecats and stoats. Stoats or *whittrits* are found on the Mainland and in

Muckle Roe and were introduced to Shetland during the 17th C. They are very active hunters, hunting in spurts with rest periods in between. The high energy requirement of a stoat means that it must eat one third of its body weight each day. The main prey is rabbits and the abundance of available food determines the litter size which can vary from four to thirteen. Stoats mate during the summer but the fertilised egg does not implant until seven months later, the growth of the embryo being triggered off by the higher spring temperatures.

Ferrets and polecat-ferrets are domesticated versions of the polecat. Ferrets are usually white whilst polecat-ferrets are brownish-coloured. In recent years there have been increasing reports from many parts of Shetland of these animals breeding in the wild, having escaped from captivity. As well as providing a threat to poultry, they also provide a potential threat to ground-nesting birds.

In ponds and ditches frog tadpoles are developing. Newly-hatched tadpoles have feathery external gills but when they are about a month old a fold of skin grows over these appendages. The tadpoles now breathe, as fish do, by passing oxygenated water over internal gills. After another month the hind legs appear, sprouting from small buds on either side of the tail. Up until now the tadpoles have been placid vegetarians, feeding on tiny amounts of green algae. When their hind legs have grown fully they become omnivorous, taking dead and living small animals in addition to their plant diet. At this stage the larger tadpoles are not adverse to snacking off smaller individuals.

On rocky seashores the seaweed cover is increasing and most inter-tidal organisms have moved back inshore. The prickly pink globular forms of sea urchins are often seen clinging to piers and jetties and may also be found in deep rock pools. They belong to the phylum *Echinodermata*, meaning 'spiny skinned', the members of which are all marine and include starfish and sea cucumbers. All have a five-rayed body plan, a calcareous endoskeleton and tube feet operated by a water vascular system. The common sea urchin grows to a diameter of about 10cm/4 ins and its body is encased in a series of fused calcareous plates which form the familiar 'shell' or test. The test is covered in purple-tipped moveable spines and radiating rows of tube feet which enable the urchin to move around the seabed. It feeds, using the five chisel-like teeth on the underside of the test, on seaweed scraped off the rock and small animals.

During May the number and variety of flying insects increases with the re-appearance of bees, hoverflies, bluebottles, house flies, lacewings, butterflies, moths and mayflies. Only about three species of mayfly have been recorded in Shetland. They are delicate-looking long-bodied insects with two pairs of wings, usually held above the body at rest, and two or three long tails at the end of the abdomen. The adult insects only survive for three or four days, sufficient time for the females to mate and lay their eggs in freshwater. The name of the group, *Ephemeroptera*, means 'short-lived'. A mayfly spends up to three years of its life as an aquatic nymph in fast-flowing well-oxygenated streams. The nymph has six sharply-hooked legs to prevent it being swept away and can be recognised as a mayfly larva by the three distinctive tails.

The south easterly winds which often bring in good 'falls' of migrant birds also can bring in other migrants from Europe. Silver Y moths are regularly recorded this month. These medium-sized moths fly by day and are readily attracted to light traps or lighted windows at night. The forewings are greyish-brown tinged with purple and in the centre of each wing is a silver Y-shaped mark composed of a series of metallic scales. The hindwings are greyish-brown with a darker scalloped band around the margins.

Trees and shrubs are coming into leaf. The emerging spring leaves are thin and almost translucent as they are designed for maximum photosynthetic efficiency. However, as the season progresses the number of plant-eating insects increases. The initial fresh-looking thin leaves are particularly vulnerable to insect attack so the plant produces leaves with higher levels of tannin. Tannins make the leaves more indigestible. These later leaves are thicker and darker in appearance, and discourage attacks by the growing hordes of leaf-munching insects.

Depending on temperatures, more plants come into flower in May. The primroses, which first appeared last month, are known as the 'may flooer' in Shetland and continue to brighten up cliffs, banks and roadsides. The cheerful golden flowers of dandelions appear in gardens, wasteground and along grassy verges. Masses of glowing marsh marigolds add colour to the slowly-greening landscape. Other species flowering this month generally include lady's smock, silverweed, red dead nettle, heath milkwort, tormentil, meadow buttercup, bird's foot trefoil, lousewort, kidney vetch, heath-spotted orchid and red campion.

Violets are also favourite symbols of spring and these low-growing perennials also begin flowering in May. Three species are native to Shetland. The commonest is the common dog violet, *Viola riviniana,* which grows in a variety of habitats – rough pasture, heathland, grassy area, heather moorland and sea cliffs. The heart-shaped leaves have long stalks and at the base of

Tormentil

each leaf stock is a pair of small scales fringed with long slender teeth. The flowers are a delicate blue-violet with a pale whitish-grey hollow curved tube or spur at the base of the petals. The marsh violet, *Viola palustris,* is found, as it name implies, growing in bogs, marshes and damp heathland. The leaves are kidney-shaped and the flower stalks have small opposite bracts about mid-way up the length. The flowers are a pale lilac veined with purple and have short spurs. The third species of violet is much rarer, found mainly on the serpentine heaths of Unst. The heath dog violet, *Viola canina,* has deep blue flowers with yellow spurs.

By the end of May there are only three weeks before mid-summer. As spring gives way to the first month of the northern summer June heralds a period of frantic activity in the natural world.

─ IN ─

June

Singest of summer in full-throated ease.

John Keats

In June the Shetland landscape reverberates with summer sounds. This is the high point in the yearly calendar – not only because it brings mid-summer, but also because June is the peak of the breeding season. The month is named in honour of Juno, the wife of Jupiter, the most important and powerful god in Roman mythology. June is regarded as the first month of summer although the weather can be cool and unsettled. However temperatures are increasing and rainfall decreasing.

It is also the month of the 'simmer-dim', the increasing hours of daylight culminating on the 21st, mid-summer, in the longest day when the sun rises at 03.42 and sets at 22.24. The sun is thus above the horizon for almost nineteen hours. If the sky is clear then the extended twilight between sunset and sunrise means that it never gets properly dark. On fine June evenings it is possible to read newsprint outdoors at midnight!

Birds are also affected by the long daylight hours, singing well into summer evenings and starting again in the early hours of the morning. The seabird cliffs produce their own chorus – drawn-out bass growls from the auks, shrill 'kittee-wake' calls, yelps from the gulls, the background cackling of fulmars and soprano peeps from newly-hatched chicks. Most cliff nesters are either still incubating or tending young this month.

Guillemot chicks hatch out on the densely crowded ledges and are fed by their parents. To avoid any wastage the adult regurgitates fish directly into the open beak of the chick. Unable to move far, the chick virtually stands still and puts all its energy into growing in preparation for its premature departure from the cliffs. Both guillemot and razorbill chicks leave the ledges when they are about three weeks old and complete their development at sea. Departure takes place after sunset to try and minimise predation. It is an amazing sight as these tiny flightless chicks, only about one third adult size, jump from the ledges and flutter down to the sea on stubby wings calling loudly. They are encouraged to take the plunge by the adults and quickly swim away from the cliffs accompanied by the male parent.

During June most puffins will still be incubating, the chicks hatching towards the end of the month or in early July. The puffin lays a very large egg in relation to the size of the adult. The egg is laid in a small chamber, lined with a few feathers and some dry vegetation, near the end of the burrow. The nest chamber is often constructed slightly higher than the burrow passage which may improve drainage. Both sexes share incubation, the incubating bird carefully tucking the egg

47

under its body and holding it against one of the brood patches. The incubation period is about six weeks which ensures that the chick is well developed when it hatches.

Puffin

Gull colonies are in full swing now, the penetrating thin cries of the chicks mingling with the wailing of the adults. Gull chicks leave the nest soon after hatching and are fed by their parents. When the adult appears the chicks peck at the red spot on the lower mandible of its beak. This stimulates the parent to regurgitate a meal for its hungry offspring. Kittiwakes also belong to the gull family but raise their chicks on precarious cliff sites. Their chicks remain in the nest until they have fledged and are fed by direct regurgitation. By the end of June some kittiwake chicks have hatched and are closely brooded for the first few days.

Throughout the islands birds are tending their broods. The eggs of small perching birds such as starling, blackbird, house sparrow, skylark, wheatear and meadow pipit have short incubation periods of around two weeks. The chicks hatch blind and featherless and, at first, are brooded continuously by the parent to keep warm. They can do little except respond to a need for food. After a few days they can be left alone for short periods. When the parent returns to the nest the chicks stretch up their heads, beaks agape. The most insistent chick is usually fed so that, in times of shortage, the strongest will survive. These nestlings grow quickly putting on fat and acquiring feathers so that they can regulate their own body temperature. They leave the nest two weeks after hatching but are generally still fed by their parents for another three weeks. The fledglings are inexperienced fliers and often fall prey to predators such as domestic cats.

The eggs of birds such as gulls, skuas, terns, waders and waterfowl are often intricately marked to blend in with the breeding habitat and are incubated for between three and four weeks. Ringed plover, which commonly nest on shingle beaches, lay four beautifully speckled eggs which look like small pebbles. Wader chicks hatch clad in soft down in shades of black, silver, brown and grey. Leaving the nest, they rely on their cryptic colouration for protection. On the approach of a potential predator the adults take to the wing calling loudly, the young responding to the alarm calls by crouching motionless. The parents may also feign injury in an attempt to lure a predator away from their chicks. Skuas, gulls and terns are more militant, favouring all out attack to protect their young.

Shetland's rarest wader is also breeding this month. Around 36 pairs of red-necked phalaropes, almost the entire British population, breed on the island of Fetlar and can be observed at the RSPB (Royal Society for the Protection of Birds) Mires of Funzie Reserve. This small elegant Arctic wader returns to Shetland in the second half of May and is unusual in that the female is dominant during the breeding season. She is brighter coloured than the male and slightly larger. The female has a slate-grey head and upper parts, brownish wings, a white throat and underparts and bright orange-red patches on the neck. Males are similarly patterned but much duller. After laying the eggs, the female red-necked phalarope takes no part in rearing the young. The male is solely responsible for incubation and looks after the chicks when they hatch. Meanwhile, the female finds another male, produces a second clutch, and then leaves him to rear her second family. Red-necked phalaropes have slender needle-like bills and feed mainly on insects and aquatic larvae.

Bird migration continues into June but becomes more sporadic in the second half of the month. The occurrence of migrants is of course highly dependent on the weather. However species regularly recorded at this time of year include whitethroat, lesser whitethroat, wryneck, common rosefinch, swallow, house martin, swift, and willow, garden, sedge and sub-alpine warblers.

Hedgehogs are courting this month. Courtship in hedgehogs is a prolonged and noisy affair with much snorting and snuffling. The male finds the female by scent and begins to circle her. The female pivots around the centre of the circle and may occasionally butt the male on the flank producing even louder snorts from her amorous would-be suitor. Sometimes the noise attracts other males which are butted out of the way by the dominant male. This can go on for hours until either the male gives up or the female is willing to mate. Mating is rarely witnessed but it is a tricky business, made slightly easier by the female arching her back and flattening her spines. Gestation lasts about thirty four days.

Otter cubs are born in early summer. The female chooses a suitable holt or *hadd* in which she gives birth, usually to one or two cubs. Although fully furred, otter cubs are born blind and helpless and remain in the holt for the first ten weeks. During this time the mother suckles them, only leaving the den to snatch a quick meal for herself. The cubs develop slowly, opening their eyes at around a month old and tottering around the den when seven to eight weeks. At this stage the mother begins weaning and encourages them to defaecate outside the den entrance.

When the cubs are about three months old, and fully weaned, the female introduces them to the sea. At first the cubs are reluctant to enter this strange watery world and the female has to encourage or coerce her offspring into, what will become, their natural element. When I was a child living in Orkney my family brought up an otter cub. At first she regarded immersion in the sea as something to be avoided. I remember my father wading out from the shore holding this squirming cub before releasing it a short distance offshore. The cub then swam ashore protesting vociferously. Our otter, like those in the wild, soon acclimatised and learned to swim, dive and forage offshore for fish and crabs.

Rocky seashores are reaching their summer peak now with countless young organisms establishing themselves. This is the predominant type of coastal habitat in Shetland but the diversity of seashore life present varies according to the degree of exposure to wave action and the geological characteristics of the rock. The beaches richest in life are those of softer rock with a gentle slope and an irregular shore profile broken up by large boulders and rocky ridges. These beaches develop a thick seaweed cover which acts as a protection against wave action and the effects of exposure.

Organisms living on seashores occupy an extremely vulnerable environment, dominated by the twice-daily tidal rhythms. The effects of the tides divide up the seashore into a series of zones, determined by the length of time each horizontal section is exposed by the receding tide. Species of seaweeds and inter-tidal animals occur in different zones depending on their adaptations to exposure or submergence.

Freshwater organisms within a pond also live in a series of overlapping zones. Nutrient-rich freshwaters are not very common in Shetland, but where they do occur, freshwater life is also reaching a peak in June. Around the edges of the pond is a zone of emergent vegetation with tall grasses, rushes and flowering plants such as yellow flag and meadowsweet. This vegetation provides valuable cover for breeding wildfowl and waders, and also for otters. Many insects have aquatic larvae which crawl up the waterside vegetation before pupating and emerging as flying adults. Growing in deeper water are plants with floating leaves and those with shoots and flowers emerging above the surface. At the surface of the pond the water molecules are strongly attracted to each other producing an 'elastic skin'. This surface film supports the weight of some specially adapted insects such as water crickets.

The open water zone has a variety of free-swimming animals such as tiny protozoa, water fleas water mites, water beetles and water boatmen. Submerged plants, like pondweed and water milfoil, provide underwater jungles for water snails, caddisfly larvae and insect nymphs. In stagnant ponds the bottom is often covered in a mud or silt which harbours species of nematodes, flatworms and insect nymphs.

As the weather becomes warmer more species of flying insects appear. 'Shetland' bumble bees or moss-carder bees buzz lazily around the garden. This common species of bumblebee is readily identified by its orangy-red thorax and unstriped yellowish abdomen. Bees are beneficial insects as they pollinate flowering plants.

Greater Water Boatman

Hoverflies should also be welcomed by the gardener. In addition to the adults acting as pollinators, the larvae are avid consumers of greenfly. Many species mimic the warning striped colouration of bees and wasps to protect them from predators. However, some do not display warning colouration such as *Rhingia campestris,* or the long-nosed hoverfly, which has an orange-brown pointed abdomen with a central black stripe. As the name 'hoverfly' suggests these insects are capable of darting hovering flight. Over twenty species have been recorded in Shetland.

June brings a mass flowering of wild flowers with fields glowing yellow with buttercups and marsh marigolds or spangled in whites, blues, pinks and purples. Even fields of humble daisies *en masse* can look stunning. Roadside verges throughout the islands become riots of colour, especially the sandy machair around Sumburgh airport which produces amazing displays of purple vetch mingled with red clover, bird's foot trefoil and eyebright.

The coastline, where protected from grazing animals, also produces spectacular flowering displays. In some places sea pink or thrift covers large areas in a bright pink honey-scented carpet. Sea pink is found on cliffs, stacks, foreshores, salt marshes, cliff tops and growing in coastal grassy areas. It has long roots which anchor the plant securely and absorb available water. On sea cliffs it finds a foot-hold in pockets of soil and can withstand exposure to salt spray. Other species which are common on Shetland seacliffs include scurvy grass, roseroot, sea campion, sea mayweed, red campion, sea plantain, curled dock and red fescue grass.

Sea Campion

Heather moorlands and rough grazings are also transformed by splashes of colour. The tiny four-petalled yellow flowers of tormentil dot the heather like tiny stars. In nineteenth century Shetland the roots were used in the tanning of leather. The name 'tormentil' comes from its past use as a powerful medicinal herb. The roots boiled in milk, were used to treat the torment of stomach ache or toothache. Also small but brightly coloured are the sapphire flowers of heath milkwort. The name comes from a belief that consumption of these plants increased milk flow in animals. Even smaller are the white flowers of heath bedstraw. All bedstraws have trailing squarish stems and the leaves are borne in whorls. Another typical moorland species is the heath- spotted orchid. The pale pink, sometimes white, flowers have small crimson spots and the leaves are dark-spotted.

June is also the best month to visit the unique plant communities growing on the serpentine debris soils of Unst. The Keen of Hamar is a National Nature Reserve, owned by Scottish Natural Heritage, where a number of plant species occur which have a restricted distribution in the rest of Britain. The upper part of the Keen is covered in small angular fragments of serpentine whilst the lower slopes support patches of well-vegetated serpentine heathland. The area is a virtual desert due to excessive drainage through the coarse stony soil.

Rare species growing here include Norwegian sandwort, a national rarity, northern rock cress and Edmonston's chickweed, an endemic sub-species of Arctic mouse-ear chickweed. Other more common species are also found which show distinctive growth forms such as thicker leaves, greater hairiness and paler flowers such as scurvy grass, sea plantain, stone bramble and thrift. Growing on the small areas of serpentine heath vegetation are moonwort, slender St John's wort, kidney vetch, frog orchid, early purple orchid, thyme, moss campion, fairy flax, mountain everlasting and heath dog violet.

Edmonston's Chickweed

As the year moves past the mid-point, the activity of the breeding season continues for most species and many wild plants are still to flower.

IN
July

And the sun went down, and the stars came out far over the summer sea.

Alfred, Lord Tennyson

July is named after Julius Caesar. In Shetland it is a month of long bright summer evenings when islands lie sharply etched against the tranquillity of sea and sky. Calm evenings can bring spectacular sunsets with sparkling red-yellow sun pillars thrown across the sea or reflected marbled pink-orange clouds shading into beautifully delicate blues and greens near the horizon. The month is generally warm and dry and vegetation lush. The end of July marks a turning point in our summer. At the start of the month most birds are still rearing young but by the end many are gathering into post-breeding flocks.

Chick-rearing continues on the seabird cliffs during the first part of July. Some guillemots and razorbills are usually still present tending their small penguin-like chicks. Further down the cliff are the large sprawling nests of shags. They have a prolonged breeding season and, whilst many have downy youngsters, others will still be incubating.

Kittiwake chicks will be visible now. Unlike the vociferous chicks of other gulls the young kittiwakes sit quietly, heads facing towards the cliff face, to minimise the chances of an accidental fatal tumble. They fledge in the nest, acquiring a distinctive adult-like plumage with a V-shaped dark band on each wing, a black tail band and a dark stripe along the nape of the neck. Although two eggs are laid, only one chick fledges on average. In recent years the breeding success has caused concern with some areas producing no fledged young. During the 1980s this species was affected by the shortage of suitably-sized sandeels. However, in the absence of food shortage problems, the main factor responsible for the decline in the production of young kittiwakes appears to be predation by bonxies.

The first gannet chicks appear in June but many more hatch this month. Although gannets are now well established at four colonies in Shetland, the first records of nesting birds only date from early this century. Breeding on Noss was first recorded in 1911, and on Vesta Skerry, off the northern tip of Unst, in 1917. A boat trip to the cliffs of Noss NNR (National Nature Reserve) provides an excellent opportunity to view the gannet colony. As the boat wallows in the slight swell, the carunculated cliffs tower above with ascending tiers of whitened ledges. Pungent wafts of guano drift downwards to mingle with the briny smell of the sea and all around are the sepulchral calls of the gannets. On the terraced ledges each pair occupy a substantial nest, often festooned with pieces of plastic twine and other debris, built just out of beak range of the nearest neighbours. These nests are used year after year.

The newly hatched chicks are covered in black leathery skin with protruding tufts of white wispy feathers and are closely brooded by the parents for the first three weeks. The chicks grow rapidly on a diet of semi-digested regurgitated fish and, by the age of four weeks, they have acquired a coat of dense white down. However gannet chicks are particularly vulnerable to cold wet weather until they are about six weeks old. They are now too large to be brooded by the parent and, if their downy feathers become sodden, the chick may be unable to maintain its body temperature and subsequently die. As it grows the chick takes a more active part in being fed and starts to beg from the returning parents, taking whole small fish from the parent's crop. The chicks are fed about twice a day.

From mid-July fulmar chicks start hatching. Other petrel eggs, such as those of the storm petrel, are still to hatch. Hidden deep inside burrows and crevices, tiny storm petrels, are incubating a single egg. Storm petrels are the smallest of the British seabirds, being slightly larger than a sparrow, and have dark brown plumage with a distinctive white rump patch. Incubation is shared, each parent incubating for two or three days before spending time at sea feeding on zooplankton. The change over of partners occurs after darkness and one of the best places to observe these secretive seabirds in Shetland is on a special evening trip to the island of Mousa.

Mousa broch

Visiting the island by day there is little evidence of 'stormies' although they breed in many of the stone dykes, the boulder beach and within the walls of the ancient well-preserved broch. Within the interior of the broch visitors may notice a musky smell or hear a strange purring sound interrupted by hiccups. However, after darkness, on calm summer evenings the scene is transformed. Waiting near the cooling-tower silhouette of the broch, the sea gleaming and the summer sky arcing above in pastel shades of pink, orange, blue and green, a dark shape suddenly materialises and swiftly disappears into the broch walls. The air is suddenly full of darting fluttering bat-like forms as the petrels arrive to change shifts with their mates. Soon it seems as if the whole island is vibrating with their churring, hiccuping calls as more and more petrels arrive. Incubation lasts for 38 to 40 days so it will be into August before the first storm petrel chicks hatch and another two months before they fledge.

Also hidden in their burrows are puffin chicks. After being brooded for the first three days of its life the puffin chick sits alone in the dark cool nest chamber whilst its parents are away fishing. The main diet consists of small shoaling fish such as sandeels, young whiting and herring. An average beakful of food is about 8 grams and the chick puts on weight rapidly. The puffin's colourful beak is a purpose-built fish-catching tool. The mandibles have inward-facing serrated edges which clamp tight on the slippery bodies of small fish. The muscular tongue is used to manoeuvre the fish into position and backward-pointing spines on the roof of the mouth ensure that the catch is held securely whilst the puffin is catching its next fish. About 60-70% of the day's food is delivered in the morning. The puffin colony then becomes quieter around the middle of the day with activity recommencing in the late afternoon and evening.

Eiders are also tending their young. After mating, the drake chooses the nesting site and accompanies the female until she begins incubating. Although some nests are on the foreshore of sheltered beaches many are a considerable distance inland. The five greenish eggs are laid in a soft nest lining of eider down plucked from the duck's breast. She incubates for about a month, carefully concealing the eggs if she has to leave the nest. The cryptic brown vermiculated plumage of the female acts as effective camouflage as she sits tight on the eggs. Soon after hatching the ducklings are usually led single-file to the sea. The tiny fluffy ducklings are extremely vulnerable to predation by gulls and skuas. The eider population in Shetland has declined from 16,500 in 1977 to around 7,000.

By the end of July there are large numbers of newly-fledged small birds such as sparrows, blackbirds, starlings, meadow pipits, skylarks and wheatears. These fledglings are particularly vulnerable to predation as they begin to move out of their parents' territories and many will not survive their first month. Survival depends on learning to fly efficiently, to find food and shelter as quickly as possible and to detect, recognise and avoid predators. Migrant fledglings also must set up their navigational systems for use in their long journeys. The birds learn how to detect north by gauging the apparent centre of rotation of the stars in the night sky.

Many waders such as oystercatcher and curlew have raised their broods and start to gather in post-breeding flocks. The first turnstones return from the Arctic having completed their breeding season. A few non-breeders remain around the Shetland coastline throughout the summer. At this time of year the turnstone has a chestnut back, white head and underparts and distinctive black marking on the face and breast.

This is the pupping season for common seals. The pregnant females haul out on a secluded beach or skerry to give birth to a single dark-coated pup. Common seal pups can swim from birth, usually following just behind their mothers. They are suckled underwater and quickly grow on a diet of rich nutritious seal milk. The females are vigilant mothers, encouraging the pups to swim to the safety of deeper water if there is any threat to their well being. However, in rough sea conditions the pair may become separated.

Every summer young common seals are found apparently abandoned. Usually the female will return and it is only if the pup is left for more than 48 hours that there should be any cause for concern. The pups are weaned at around four weeks old and by six weeks they are independent, hunting and catching their own fish. Young common seals usually remain with groups of adult seals throughout the summer. After the pups are weaned the females mate, although the fertilised egg undergoes a period of delayed implantation so that the pups are born at the same time next year.

This is also a good month to observe larger sea mammals. Several species of whales and dolphins regularly visit Shetland waters during the summer months, the commonest being the harbour porpoise or *neesik* which tend to favour bays and sounds between islands. The head of the porpoise is short and blunt, unlike the characteristic pointed 'beak' of dolphins. The usual colour is dark grey above with lighter underparts. Harbour porpoises reach a length of about 1.8m/6ft, the small size and blunt triangular dorsal fin being diagnostic features. They travel in small groups and eat a varied diet of fish, crustaceans and cuttlefish.

Killer whales are also frequently seen during the summer months. These strikingly patterned black and white whales travel in pods of varying sizes. The colouration is mainly black on the upperparts and white beneath, with lobes of the white extending upwards on either flank and white patches behind the eyes. At the base of the dorsal fin, extending backwards, is a saddle-shaped patch of grey pigmentation.

Killer Whale

The dorsal fin of the larger adult males is a distinctive feature, rising to 1.8m/5ft 10ins. Pods consist of an adult male, several adult females and a number of sub-adults of both sexes. Members of the pod show a high degree of co-operation in hunting, the prey ranging from fish and squid to birds, seals and even other whales.

Tadpoles are starting to metamorphose into frogs now. The hind legs develop first and, when these are well grown, the forelegs quickly appear. Their speedy appearance is due to being hidden by a flap of skin which formed over the gills. This disappears as the internal gills are replaced by lungs in the maturing tadpole. The colour of the skin changes to a speckled grey-green and the body tapers sharply at the join of the hind legs. The head also starts to become more frog-like with a wide gape and the eyes become larger and more prominent. The tadpole now must make frequent trips to the surface of the pond to breathe air. Over the next few weeks the tail is gradually absorbed into the body and the tadpole becomes a tiny froglet.

Sandy beaches are popular in summer. Although there is usually some evidence of the inhabitants the permanent residents, mainly bivalve molluscs and worms, live buried beneath the surface of the sand. Common bivalves living on sandy or muddy shores include tellins, striped venus, razorshells, cockles, carpet shells, trough shells and sand gapers. These either feed by filtering out small edible particles from currents of sea water, such as cockles, or by sucking up organic detritus and diatoms from the surface of sand with long siphons like tellins. Worms either feed, like lugworms, by passing sand through their bodies and extracting edible particles or by filtering out food from sea water, such as sand mason worms or are active predators like ragworms.

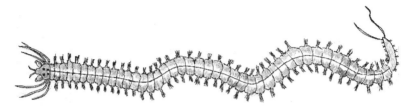

Ragworm

Butterflies are a feature of July, the commonest species being large whites, which are resident in the islands, and red admirals, which are migrants. Red admirals originate from warmer regions around the Mediterranean with the first arrivals in June and July. These may then breed and produce a local population later in the summer. Further influxes of migrant red admirals also occur throughout the summer and sometimes into the autumn. These attractive strongly-patterned butterflies are strong fliers and are attracted to gardens with nectar-rich flowers. The eggs are laid on the upper surface of the leaves of stinging nettles, the larvae spinning webs in which they feed, grow and pupate. Other migrant butterfly species recorded this month include painted lady and peacock.

Several species of moths are also recorded this month including angle shades, clouded bordered brindle, dark brocade, ingrailed clay, large yellow underwing, dark arches and ghost swift moth. The latter is a particularly large and noticeable moth, the females having orange-yellow wings and the slightly smaller males appearing a shimmering white although many Shetland specimens have brownish wing markings. Ghost moths have fore and hind wings of equal size and fat furry bodies which store reserves of energy as the adults

Female Ghost Swift Moth

do not feed. At dusk the males perform a ghostly hovering dance over grassy areas, meanwhile emitting a powerful pheromone which attracts females. The females join in this display before each pair settles on a grass stem to mate. The eggs are scattered in flight and tumble down into the base of tussocks of grass. The larvae are brown-headed whitish caterpillars which feed on plant roots and may over-winter for two years before emerging as adults.

During July there are a profusion of plant species in unimproved hay meadows. These are some of the richest botanical habitats in Shetland, some meadows containing over eighty species of flowering plants. Common species include Yorkshire fog, sweet vernal grass, clovers, tufted vetch, meadow vetchling, yellow rattle, ragged robin, eyebright, mouse-ear chickweed, northern marsh orchid and meadow buttercup.

In marshy areas and along ditches the showy yellow-orange flowers of mimulus *Mimulus guttatus* appear. This species, which originated in Alaska, was introduced to Britain in the early nineteenth century and is now widely naturalised. The intricately folded red-spotted petals look rather like a grinning face. *Mimulus* means 'little actor' and *guttatus* means 'spotted'. Yellow iris, or yellow flag is another distinctive wet-loving species which flowers in July. Known as *seggies* in Shetland, the plant grows from underground rhizomes in dense clumps and has tall sharp-edged leaves. The flowers, two to three to each stem, appear one at a time and have an intricate structure of folded yellow sepals and petals, with fringing and dark markings. Meadowsweet with its creamy sweet-scented umbels of flowers also occurs in wetland habitats. In the absence of flowers the leaves are easily identified from those of other umbellifers by the dense white hairs on the undersides. This species is native to Shetland and was once an important source of black dye.

Yellow Iris

The July moorland is transformed in some areas by sheets of burnished yellow-orange flowers. Bog asphodel, *Narthecium ossifragum*, is a common native perennial which grows from spreading underground stems. The flowers, resembling tiny stars, are borne on a spike and produce a sweet clove-like scent. After flowering the entire flower and flower stalk turn a beautiful deep orange. The *ossifragum* part of the name refers to an old belief that sheep grazing on this plant developed brittle bone disease. The ailment was probably caused by mineral deficiencies in animals pastured on the nutrient-poor habitats in which bog asphodel is found.

Two species of moorland plants supplement their nutrient intake, especially nitrates, by trapping and digesting insects. Common butterwort has a pale green starfish-like rosette of leaves which appear in late spring. The flowers are borne singly on long stalks and are bluish-violet with pale centres. The leaves are sticky and trap small insects which are then digested as the leaf curls lengthways over its victims. Later the leaf uncurls to void the inedible remains. The other insectivorous plant of the moorland is the round-leaved sundew which often blends in with the surrounding mosses. The plant is reddish with small round leaves which also form a basal rosette. Each leaf is covered in a multitude of tiny sticky hairs, each tipped with

Common Butterwort

58

a glistening droplet. Insects mistake the droplets for dew and become entangled in the sticky hairs. The leaves then curl around the insect whilst powerful enzymes liquefy the victim. The delicate flowers of the sundew are whitish but often do not open fully and are self-pollinated.

As we move into August more of the fields are cut giving the landscape in crofting areas a patchwork appearance.

S H E T L A N D

— IN —

August

And summer's green all girded up in sheaves.

William Shakespeare

Hay making in Shetland starts this month although much of the grass grown in the islands is now used for silage. As the fields are shorn, the pale yellow-green stubble contrasts with the lush green of adjacent fields. August is usually the warmest driest month with average temperatures of around 15°C . Sea temperatures peak at around 13°C, being higher in the shallow voes than in inlets with deeper water. The temperature of the sea is influenced by the distribution of water masses around the islands and by the tides. Temperatures are generally cooler on the east coast compared to the west coast. Although the weather is usually settled there are increasing signs that our short northern summer is coming to an end.

At the start of the month there is still an abundance of breeding seabirds but numbers are starting to diminish. Guillemots and razorbills have deserted the sea cliffs but can still be seen inshore. Young puffins fledge from late July onwards and by mid-August only a few adults remain around the colonies. The puffin fledgling is clad in a soft down right up until its final few days in the burrow. It then moults into adult-like black and white plumage. However the juvenile is much dowdier than its gaudy parents. The head and cheeks are dark and the small slim beak is dark grey as are the legs and feet.

The young puffin makes its final departure alone, under cover of darkness. Having cautiously emerged from the burrow and checked for potential predators, the puffling scurries to the cliff edge. After some initial hesitation, it launches itself into mid-air on its first flight. The young puffin flies awkwardly, clearing the colony, before splashing down a few hundred metres out to sea. Alternately swimming and diving, it moves further offshore away from marauding gulls and skuas. Most will not return to land again until they are at least three years old.

Tysties or black guillemots are resident in Shetland throughout the year and their young also fledge in August. Breeding tysties favour low rocky shorelines and offshore islands. Unlike other auks, they lay two eggs, usually in crevices or under large rocks. The chicks are fed on small inshore fish such as butterfish and remain at the nesting site until they have fledged. Young tysties look like adults in winter plumage but are darker in colour and have brown mottling on the white wing patch. At the end of the breeding season the adults gather into moult flocks and become flightless for a time.

Throughout August gannets and shags still have young in the nest at different stages of development. Fulmar chicks, which started hatching out in mid-July, also remain at the nest site for about eight weeks so are present throughout this month. The newly-hatched chicks are clad in a soft grey down and resemble large powder-puffs as they squat at the nest sites. They are fed by both parents, the liquefied food being pumped directly into the chick's beak. Older chicks are left alone at the nest site whilst the parents forage at sea. However, if an intruder approaches too closely the innocuous-looking 'powder-puff' chick will regurgitate a stream of vile-smelling fishy oil as a deterrent. Ringing fulmar chicks is a smelly business!

On moorland lochs red-throated divers also have well-grown chicks. The two eggs are laid in a vegetation-lined scrape by the loch. The nest is sited very close to the water's edge so that the incubating bird can enter the water easily and unobtrusively. Red-throats are virtually helpless on land as their body is designed for diving and swimming. The powerful webbed feet and legs, designed for maximum downward propulsion, are situated far back on the body which means movement on land is awkward and laborious. The location of the nest makes it vulnerable to changes in the loch water levels. A drought causes the level to drop creating a longer more dangerous route between the nest and the safety of the loch, whilst heavy rainfall can cause flooding with subsequent egg loss if the level of the loch rises dramatically.

An added problem is that red-throats are easily disturbed from their nests thus exposing the eggs to predation. Red-throated divers are fully protected by current conservation legislation. However their vulnerability during the breeding season has lead to a worrying decrease in breeding success over the last ten years. The number of breeding pairs has decreased from around 700 in 1983 to just over 420 in 1994.

The adults fly down to the sea to catch fish offshore for the growing chicks. After hatching, the chicks remain in the nest for about a day before following the adults into the water. Two chicks are generally produced but often only one will survive. Fledging takes six weeks and the fully-grown young leave the lochs in late August/early September. Some red-throats winter around Shetland but most disperse southwards.

The bird which epitomises heather moorland in Scotland and is strongly associated with August, is scarce in Shetland. Red grouse occur mainly in parts of the Central and South Mainland with a few pairs on Yell. They were introduced to the islands by nineteenth century landlords for sporting purposes, the last introduction being 600 birds at Lunna in 1901. However the population remains small, possibly because of the comparatively poor rate of heather growth, a plant essential in all stages of the grouse's life cycle, and competition with sheep. The plump shape, dark red-brown plumage, red combs, fast strong flight and characteristic call make identification

Red Grouse

easy. Often the first sign of the bird is when it explodes upwards from cover on rapidly whirring wings. Grouse chicks fledge quickly so, by August, the juveniles are also on the wing.

Young mammals, such as hedgehogs, are becoming independent this month. Hedgehogs are born thoughout the summer. After being suckled in the nest for the first three weeks, the female starts leading them out each night on hunting expeditions. The young soon learn to feed themselves and become independent by the time they are six weeks old. Any hedgehogs born this month will have a poorer chance of survival for it will be a race against time for them to gain enough weight to survive the winter.

Otter cubs are still with their mothers but can swim and hunt with ease. Even during the summer when there are more people about, it is possible to see otters during the day. One hot August day we watched an interesting encounter between a dog otter and two common gulls. He was hunting in a shallow lagoon, peppered with small irregularly-shaped grassy islets, separated by a shingle beach from the sea. The otter systematically explored the peripheries of several of the islets, occasionally coming ashore in a gleam of spiked fur to roll ecstatically on the vegetation. Submerging beneath rafts of yellow-brown knotweed, he emerged with seaweed draped over his head like a rakish mantilla, his gleaming canines making short work of his catch.

His hunting forays brought him nearer to the mouth of the lagoon where two common gulls were perching. The gulls immediately began mobbing the otter, swooping hysterically each time he surfaced. Even after the otter crossed the shingle beach and entered the sea he was pursued unrelentingly by the swooping attacks and vituperative screeches of the gulls. He continued fishing close inshore but each time he came to the surface the gulls renewed their onslaught. Eventually he swam away from the shore and dived, leaving behind a glittering wake and two annoyed gulls.

There is also a chance of seeing a much larger mammal in Shetland waters this month. Over the last few years there have been increasing reports of minke whales. Most sightings occur between July and

Minke Whale

September and are most frequent on the east side of Shetland. Minke whales, known as *herring hogs* to Shetland fishermen, are the smallest of the baleen whales reaching lengths of 9.4m/31ft for females and 8.2m/27ft for males. The dorsal fin is small and slightly curved and the colouration is generally dark grey above and white below. Baleen whales feed by filtering out plankton from the seawater using fringed horny plates within the mouth.

A common sight in inshore waters in late summer are large numbers of jellyfish. The most abundant species is the moon jellyfish *Aurelia aurita*, identified by the four horseshoe-shaped structures, part of its reproductive system, embedded in the transparent bell. The largest species is the yellow-orange lion's mane, *Cyanea capillata*, often seen in deep waters off cliffs or stranded in a jelly-like lump on the beach. The lion's mane can grow up to 1m/3ft across with long stinging tentacles, up to 12m/40ft in length, trailing beneath the bell. These tentacles are used in catching small fish and can inflict a painful sting on the unwary. *Cyanea lamarcki* is a beautiful deep blue-violet colour and is also common in Shetland waters.

Close relatives of jellyfish, sea gooseberries or comb jellies, may also be observed inshore. Comb jellies are basically transparent sacs of jelly which are powered by eight rows of comb-like plates of cilia. Their true beauty is revealed when the moving cilia cause iridescent rainbow colours to pulse along their bodies. They are carnivorous, feeding on small animals in the plankton. The species most likely to be encountered around Shetland is *Beroë cucumis*.

The warm humid nights of August are good for sugaring to attract moths. A sugar solution is made up by heating dark brown sugar, treacle, beer and rum to a syrup-like consistency, allowing it to cool, and then adding a few drops of pear essence. Before dusk the mixture is painted onto various vertical sites such as fence posts. After dark each sugared site is visited with a torch and the different species of moths feeding on the mixture recorded. Often it is necessary to catch the moth for identification.

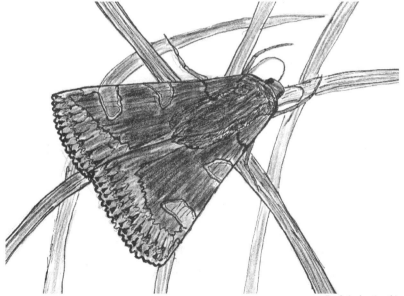

Dark Arches (moth)

One of the commonest species, attracted to both light and sugar, is the dark arches. This species is very variable ranging from pale to very dark specimens, the dark or melanistic form predominating in Shetland. It is possible that the long hours of summer daylight confer an advantage on the darker forms. The explanation may lie in some kind of physiological response to cool temperatures. The brown forewings have irregular lighter patterns, more obscured in darker specimens, whilst the hind wings are light coloured. Dark arches also have a habit of shivering their wings when at rest. Another very common species is the red carpet. This small moth is readily attracted to light, settling with both fore and hind wings spread. Across the beige coloured forewings is a wavy red band, the intensity of which varies considerably.

Other insects are also on the wing on calm, summer nights. Lacewings are delicate, attractive insects with elongated bodies, long antennae and large beautiful transparent gauzy wings which are held over the body at rest. The species commonly recorded in Shetland is the green lacewing, *Chrysoperia carnea*,

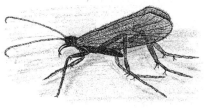
Caddisfly

which has a pale green body, becoming pinker in the autumn. They are generally recorded from July onwards but do not appear to be able to overwinter successfully. The larvae are avid eaters of aphids.

Caddisflies are also hatching out at this time of the year and many are attracted to lighted windows. These are medium-sized brownish insects with delicate veined wings which are held roof-wise over the body. The eyes are large and the antennae long and slender. They are weak fliers, most of their life being spent as aquatic larvae. Caddisfly larvae protect themselves by constructing tiny cases of vegetation, tiny stones or small shells around their soft bodies, the pattern of each case being specific to each species. After about a year the larva pupates and, after another few weeks, the pupa crawls out of water and up the stem of a water plant. The pupal skin splits and the adult caddisfly emerges. It lives for about a month after emergence.

During August the moorland becomes suffused by a purple tinge as ling heather comes into flower. Ling is easily recognised by its tiny lilac-purple flowers which form loose spikes at the top the stem. The common name comes from an old Anglo Saxon word, *lig*, meaning fire as the dry stems catch fire easily. Ling is an evergreen dwarf shrub which lives for around thirty years. It has four distinct phases in its life cycle which are important in the ecology of heather moorlands. In the *pioneer phase*, 3-6 years, the heather establishes itself and is at its most nutritious. From 6-15 years it is in the *building phase* when most of the growth is in the short shoots, the long shoots growing out sideways so that the plant begins to assume a dome-shape. It then enters the *mature phase* until it is 20-25 years old when the long shoots grow less vigorously and it reaches its maximum height. Stands of mature heather provide important cover for mountain hares and breeding birds, such as the merlin. Sometime between 25-30 years old the heather plant reaches the *degenerate phase* when a gap appears in the centre of the clump and the remaining branches lie prostrate. The centre gap increases in size and gradually the whole plant dies.

Other dwarf shrubs are also flowering in moorland and heathland areas. Bell heather, *Erica cinerea*, grows in drier conditions and produces purple-pink bell-shaped flowers which are clustered at the top of the stem. The leaves are tiny and glossy, each with a tightly rolled edge to reduce water loss. Cross-leaved heath has pink flowers of a similar shape and size but favours wet boggy moorland. The leaves are arranged in whorls of four at intervals along the stem, appearing like a cross when viewed from above. Another woody plant found on moorland is crowberry or 'berry heather'. The slender sprawling stems are red when the plant is young and become browner with age. In August small black berries are produced which are an important food source for moorland birds. They can be made into jam but are rather tart if eaten raw. In some hill top areas bilberry, *Vaccinium myrtillus*, can be found which produces sweet black berries with a delicate blue-grey bloom.

Ling

Although many flowering plants are over by August, many more are just starting to flower. Grassy areas support later-flowering species such as self heal, devil's-bit, autumnal hawkbit, yarrow and angelica. Self heal is a short-growing perennial with two-lipped purple flowers which was widely used as a healing herb in medieval times. Devil's-bit was also used as a medicinal herb, the name referring to the appearance of the root which looks as though it has been bitten off. According to legend, the devil bit off part of the root in an attempt to curtail the healing powers of this plant. It has tough elongate leaves from which arise stems bearing the purple-blue flowerheads composed of tiny four-petalled flowers.

Red campion is a common and showy species which has a long flowering period, May-early September. The flower colour can be very variable ranging from palest pink to a deep rich magenta. This species is found in a variety of habitats including grassy seacliffs (especially those enriched by seabird guano), beaches, quarries, roadsides and by stone dykes and streams. Some of the coastal specimens, particularly those growing on sandstone seacliffs, have been characterised as belonging to the sub-species *zetlandicum*. These plants have slightly larger magenta flowers crowded in a dense terminal cluster and larger seeds. Red campion belongs to the pink family and each of the five petals are deeply cleft. Each flower is either male or female. The centre of the male flowers have an inner ring within which the yellow pollen-bearing tips of the stamens can be seen. The female flowers have five feathery white stigmas protruding from the centre. After the female flowers are fertilised an oval green seed capsule forms which gradually hardens and turns light brown. Within this capsule are quantities of small black seeds.

By the end of August most of the seabirds have left the cliffs and the breeding season is almost over for most species. The Shetland countryside starts to take on a definite 'hairst' look as the remaining hay is harvested and the grass starts to brown and wither.

————— IN —————

September

I saw old autumn in the misty morn
Stand shadowless like silence, listening
To silence.

Thomas Hood

September can bring an 'Indian summer' with warm sunny weather. In the calm hazy days the shades of green in the landscape gradually change to ochres and beiges, whilst the leaves on trees and shrubs develop the familiar reds, yellows and oranges of autumn. However, sometimes the first autumn gale arrives this month blackening and shrivelling the remaining vegetation and tearing the leaves from the trees. As the month progresses the northern hemisphere begins to tilt further away from the sun and wildlife prepare to face the coming decreases in daylight, temperature and food abundance.

Most seabirds have completed their breeding season and departed, although a few gannet chicks are still fledging at the beginning of September. After an average of ninety days in the nest the young are about 30% heavier than the adults, weighing around 4.5kg/10lb, and spend much of their time wing flapping to strengthen their wing muscles for flight. However, on departure from the nest site the juveniles are too heavy to fly effectively. They fly a short distance from the breeding cliffs and then swim southwards, living on their fat reserves for one or two weeks, whilst learning how to catch shoaling fish. Many of these young gannets will starve if they are forced to use up much of their reserves combating cold weather and rough seas. As the young bird loses weight and its wings develop fully, it takes to the air and starts learning how to plunge dive for prey. At this time of year juvenile gannets may sometimes be found ashore, even appearing inland. Gannets which fledge early have the best chance of success, and by mid-September most of the young birds have left the breeding cliffs.

Most guillemots and razorbills have moved away from the islands by now but a few may be observed inshore. Guillemots in winter plumage have white cheeks and throats with a dark line behind the eyes although the crown of the head remains brownish-black. Razorbills also develop white throats and cheeks but retain brownish feathering around the eyes and can also be distinguished from guillemots by their large laterally-flattened bills. The juveniles of both these auks resemble the adults in winter plumage but have smaller bills. Adult tysties have also exchanged their glossy black summer plumage for the grey and white of their winter dress. They retain the characteristic white wing patch and red legs.

Male eiders have been gathering in large moult flocks since late June, becoming flightless for part of the time. They moult out of their smart breeding plumage into blotchy brown and white eclipse feathering, completing the moult by the end of September. Moult flocks congregate in specific areas, usually near remote headlands and uninhabited islands. During the winter eiders disperse all around the islands, flocks often gathering over soft sandy or muddy shores to feed on mussels and crabs. Prey is caught by diving underwater to depths of over 30m/100ft.

Throughout September passage and wintering waders are arriving. One of the most important sites in Shetland for wader-watching is the Pool of Virkie, near Sumburgh in the South Mainland. The tide recedes to reveal a shallow tidal basin with exposed areas of sand and mudflats, rich in invertebrates. The best time to visit is about two hours before high tide as the feeding waders are moving towards the observer, ahead of the incoming tide. Resident species which may be observed include curlew, redshank, ringed plover and dunlin whilst migrants such as knot, grey plover, little stint, curlew sandpiper, ruff, bar-tailed godwit, spotted redshank, greenshank, wood and green sandpipers are regularly recorded.

Sanderling

Waders divide up mudflats into a series of niches, depending on the length of their bills. Small wading birds, such as the ringed plover, have short bills and specialise on small shrimps, crabs and molluscs which live on the surface of the muddy sand. The plover scurries along the mud, spies its prey, stops, tilts its body forward to eat and then hurries on. This run-stop-peck technique is characteristic of feeding plovers. Sanderling, passage migrants from the Arctic, also display distinctive feeding behaviour. These waders stay close to the edge of the sea on sandy beaches. As a wave recedes they dash down the beach on twinkling legs following the retreating water. Snatching the food item left on the surface of the wet sand, they scurry up the beach again like silver-grey clockwork toys.

Medium-sized waders, like dunlin and redshank, use touch-sensitive slender bills to detect their prey. Probing a short distance down into the sand, about 5cm/2ins, they detect the presence of shallowly-buried sandhoppers, shrimps, molluscs and worms. The larger waders, such as curlew and bar-tailed godwit, use a similar technique but they can reach much further down, to depths of up to 16cm/6 ins. This enables them to feed on larger invertebrates buried in the sand like ragworms, lugworms and cockles. By feeding on these larger prey these waders can spend less time feeding than the smaller probing species. Research has shown that a curlew only needs to spend 47% of the tidal cycle feeding compared to the 75% required by a dunlin.

Other familiar waders leave Shetland in the autumn. Most of the oyster-catcher population have departed to estuaries on the Scottish mainland although a large number of birds in transit may be recorded at the Pool of Virkie in September. During the late autumn and winter months a small flock of oystercatchers generally remain around this area and at Clickimin in Lerwick. Whimbrel and red-necked phalarope have left the islands by now whilst golden plover and lapwing congregate in large nomadic flocks feeding along the coastline and in the fields.

Lapwing

As summer visitors depart the first of the winter visitors start to arrive. Waterfowl which breed further north migrate to winter in the comparatively mild climate of Shetland. Resident mallards, emerging from eclipse plumage by the end of the month, are joined by visiting birds which swell the local populations. Flocks of tufted, goldeneye and pochard re-appear whilst the first whooper swans wing in from their breeding grounds in Iceland.

Bird migrants, on passage from Scandinavia, pass through Shetland this month. The autumn migration is generally a more noticeable event than the spring passage as the numbers are augmented by young birds. Also migrants tend to remain around longer during the autumn months as there is more food available, especially for seed and berry eaters. However identification can be more tricky as many individuals are in immature or worn breeding plumage. Migrants can be divided into three main categories – passage migrants, vagrants and unexpected rarities.

Passage migrants have established travel routes with recognised re-fuelling stops such as Shetland. They tend to seek out areas of cover such as clumps of trees or bushes where they can rest and feed before continuing their journey. Regularly occurring common passage migrants include willow warblers, chiffchaffs, garden warblers, lesser whitethroats, whitethroats, robins, redstarts, whinchats, blackcaps, song thrushes, house martins, pied and spotted flycatchers. Scarcer species such as red-backed shrike, wryneck, bullfinch, hawfinch, hoopoe, Richard's pipit, yellow-browed warbler, short-toed lark and barred warbler are also recorded during the autumn migration.

A vagrant is the term used for a species which has wandered or been blown away from its normal migration route. These include species such as greenish warbler, Arctic warbler, rose-coloured starling, citrine wagtail, pechora pipit, lanceolated warbler, olive-backed pipit, Pallas' grasshopper warbler, yellow-breasted and ortolan buntings. Unexpected rarities are species which occasionally appear thousands of miles outside their normal breeding ranges or migration routes. Examples which have occurred in Shetland include red-flanked bluetail, Swainson's thrush, Blyth's pipit, Siberian rubythroat, chestnut and pine buntings.

Whooper Swans (silhouettes)

Most mammals have ceased breeding by now and many of this year's offspring are seeking out and establishing their own territories and home ranges. Young otters remain with their mothers, usually taking a year before they become independent. However young rabbits, mountain hares, hedgehogs, stoats and rodents are all on their own now. There are three species of rodent in Shetland – the brown rat, house mouse and long-tailed fieldmouse. The most attractive of these is the long-tailed fieldmouse or *hill mouse*.

At this time of year fieldmice move closer to crofts and houses, sometimes taking up residence within buildings, taking advantage of the seeds in hay 'desses' and oat 'stooks' on inbye land. They are attractive little animals, distinguished from the greyer house mouse by having larger ears and reddish fur on the back set off by whitish underparts. It is thought that these mice were brought to Shetland by Norse colonists around the tenth century. The specimens found on Shetland are larger and more brightly coloured than those found on mainland Britain and are genetically more similar to fieldmice in Norway. Separate races or sub-species have evolved on the islands of Yell, Foula and Fair Isle. The larger size of Shetland fieldmice give them a physiological advantage as a larger animal is less susceptible to cold.

Offshore, cetaceans continue to be observed throughout September. Species recorded at this time of year include white-beaked and Atlantic white-sided dolphins. Dolphins are small toothed whales with the mouth parts elongated into a characteristic pointed 'beak'. The white-beaked dolphin has white on its beak, throat and belly, the forehead and back being dark-coloured. The Atlantic white-sided dolphin has pale elongated markings along the sides and whitish underparts, the rest of the body appearing blackish. Both species swim fast and exuberantly, often leaping clear of the water, earning them the Shetland fishermen's name of *looper dog*. Dolphins often play around the bow wave of ships, taking advantage of the pressure field created by the ship's bow wave to hitch an effortless ride.

A much larger marine visitor to Shetland waters in the summer and autumn is the basking shark. This large creature, reaching up to 11m/36ft in length, is the second largest fish in the sea. It swims around close to the surface with its huge mouth ominously agape but its prey are only the tiny animals and plants of the plankton. The cavernous mouth acts as a trap for the plankton-laden water which is then passed over five rows of broom-like gill rakers. Every hour the gill rakers filter 2,000 tons of water, producing about 2kg/4lb of plankton. Much remains unknown about this gentle giant such as where basking sharks go in the winter or information on mating and gestation periods.

Migratory moths continue to be caught this month. Like migrant birds, the best influxes occur when the wind is in the south east. Many moths are attracted to light and will fly to outside lights or lighted windows. However the best type of light for attracting moths is ultra-violet, used in specialised moth traps. The light source is pre-programmed to switch on after dark and switch off before sunrise. Below the ultra-violet bulb there is a funnel with a series of vanes which deflects the circling moths into the container below. The container is stacked with cardboard egg boxes amongst which the moths crawl and settle.

A common species, attracted by light, is the antler moth which has reddish-brown wings with tawny markings. Along the length of each wing there is a pale central vein which branches to produce a pattern resembling antlers. A larger showier species is the large yellow underwing. This moth has bright yellow hindwings edged with a black border and will come to sugar solution or may be found feeding on nectar-rich flowers. Another two larger species are the dark and the red sword-grass. Both species have long dark wings and are attracted to sugar but the dark sword-grass is smaller and keeps its wings flat at rest, the wings having distinctive dark markings. The red sword-grass has a wingspan of about 2.5cm/1in and, at rest, it resembles a piece of wood, the effect being enhanced by the longitudinally pleated wings.

Even larger moths are sometimes recorded around this time of year. The hawk-moths are large stout-bodied insects with narrow pointed long wings capable of swift powerful flight. The species most commonly recorded is the convolvulus hawk-moth which has a forewing length of 4.5-5cm/2ins. They are migrants from the Mediterranean region, generally arriving in Shetland during August and September. At rest, the long forewings, beautifully patterned in shades of grey and brown, are held obliquely against the sides of the body completely concealing the hindwings and abdomen. Hawk-moths are active after dusk, the forewings opening to reveal the distinctive striped abdomen with pale pink bands, edged with white, alternating with black stripes with a greyish central streak.

Calm dewy autumn mornings are a good time to observe the delicate gossamer webs of the garden spider, *Araneus diadematus*. The garden spider can be recognised by its oval body with white dots forming a cross on the back. The female is larger than the male, with an average body length of about 12mm/½in. The female spider constructs her web using silk-producing glands in her abdomen, putting in the sticky spiral last. Toothed claws on her feet coupled with an oily secretion prevents the spider sticking to her own web. The spider may sit in the hub of the web and

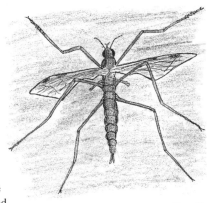

Cranefly

70

await her prey or, more often, conceals herself nearby holding a silken line attached to the web. When a flying insect becomes entangled in the web, she scuttles out and delivers a killing bite from her fangs. The victim is either eaten or wrapped in a silken cocoon for later dining.

Craneflies, sometimes known as 'daddy-long-legs', hatch in large numbers in late summer and early autumn, many finding their way into houses and buildings. They are slow fliers, preferring to crawl up windows, walls and vegetation and seem to have a fatal attraction for containers full of water. At rest the gauzy forewings are outstretched and the long gangly legs splayed out. The males have rounded swollen ends to their abdomens whilst those of the females are pointed to assist with laying eggs into the soil. The eggs hatch into grey larvae known as 'leatherjackets' or, in Shetland, *storie worms*. The larvae feed on plant roots and, on humid nights, come to the surface to eat the base of plant stems. They are extremely destructive on grassland and re-seeded areas, weakening grasses so that they are less able to withstand the winter. The larvae feed underground throughout the winter, pupating in early summer before emerging as adult craneflies.

Many plant species have finished flowering by now. Along the roadsides the umbels of hogweed are heavy with seed but another umbellifer, angelica, continues flowering until at least mid-month. It has characteristic swollen sheaths where the leaf stalks join the stem and umbrellas of whitish flowers often tinged pink-purple. The name 'angelica' comes from the angelic or heavenly properties attributed to this plant by medieval herbalists. Another late-flowering umbellifer, yarrow, was also a well known medicinal herb. The leaves are finely divided into many small and narrow segments and the whitish flowers are clustered in dense flat heads at the top of the furrowed woolly stems. Other plant species still in flower in September include thistles, sow thistles, devil's bit, eyebright, tormentil, lesser spearwort, scentless mayweed, ragwort, red dead nettle and autumnal hawkbit.

On the seashore, the fragrant flowers of sea rocket, *Cakile maritima* persist throughout the month. It grows along the strand-line on sandy and shingle beaches, especially in the South Mainland, Yell and Unst. Sea rocket is an annual with tough drought-resistant and salt-tolerant leaves which can colonise bare sand. The flowers have four petals and are a delicate shade of lilac.

By the end of September the equinox has passed and the hours of darkness again exceed those of daylight. As the year moves into October the remnants of summer make way for signs of autumn.

IN

October

O wild west wind thou breath of Autumn's being
Thou, from whose unseen presence the leaves dead
Are driven, like ghosts from an enchanter fleeing.

Percy Shelley

In some years 'wild west' winds and gales from other points of the compass strip the remaining leaves from trees and bushes. In others the leaves remain into October lending an autumnal look to parts of the islands. In the first part of the month cold weather is generally ameliorated by the warmer sea temperatures which have built up during the summer months. However, by mid-October the weather becomes more unsettled as the polar air mass moves further south towards the Shetland Islands. The weather often becomes wet and windy with an increasing likelihood of night frosts. At the end of the month evenings become artificially lengthened as we leave British Summertime behind. As the night sky begins to dominate once again the familiar winter constellation of Orion the Hunter reappears over the southern horizon.

Only the resident seabirds remain along the coastlines and cliffs – fulmar, shag, cormorant, tystie, great black-backed gull and herring gull. A few bonxies may linger on through the month before departing our shores to winter in the Atlantic Ocean. Inshore waters around the islands provide wintering grounds for great northern divers and long-tailed duck escaping the severe weather in the Arctic regions. Grey herons, visitors from Scandinavia, take up their fishing stances along the voes and sheltered shorelines like ancient heraldic emblems. More waterfowl arrive and the familiar call of the wild geese is heard again as migrating skeins trace dotted lines across the skies.

Some migrating geese remain in Shetland over the winter, especially around the Loch of Spiggie in the South Mainland, feeding on re-seeded and stubble fields and gleaning left-over potatoes. The largest and commonest of these is the greylag, the ancestor of all our domesticated geese. It is bulky in appearance with a large head, orange bill, thick neck, grey-brown plumage and pink legs. The blue-grey forewing shows up well in flight. Pink-footed geese are smaller and slimmer than greylags with darker heads and necks and blackish-pink bills. In flight they are faster than skeins of greylags and display distinctive light grey forewings. The calls are high-pitched and yelping, like a pack of small hounds. Barnacle geese are usually seen as passage migrants but small flocks may over-winter, sometimes feeding and roosting on uninhabited offshore islands. They are handsome boldly patterned geese. The head is mainly white with a contrasting black neck, grey black-barred back and white underparts. Other species which occur in Shetland include brent, Canada, white-fronted and bean geese.

Flying geese (silhouette)

Shetland has a small resident population of tufted duck which is augmented at this time of year by wintering birds from further north. Amongst the flocks there may be some scaup. This species breeds in Iceland and North Europe and small numbers pass through Shetland with a few pairs usually remaining throughout the winter. Superficially similar to tufted duck in appearance, they are slightly larger and have no crest. The male scaup can be distinguished by the pale middle section of the body flanked by a dark breast and stern. Seen at closer quarters the back is pale grey and the head is a dark glossy green. The female scaup differs from the female tufted by having a broad white band at the base of the bill. Both species are diving ducks, submerging frequently to feed on aquatic invertebrates and water plants.

The migration of thousands of passerines continues this month. Large flocks of redwings and fieldfares pass through, often thousands arriving in one influx, with many staying on several days or weeks. Attractive birds, about the size of a starling, redwings have brown upperparts and whitish, streaked underparts, displaying a rich-red flash under the wings. On the ground they have a bold creamy eyestripe and reddish feathers on the flanks. The fieldfare is a larger bulkier bird with a long tail and wings. The grey head and rump, black tail and rufous back are diagnostic features. Beneath, a rusty-buff black-streaked breast shades into whitish underparts. In flight fieldfares display white underwings whilst on the ground they adopt a characteristic upright posture with the wings drooping downward. Although both species feed on berries and seeds they also take invertebrates and are commonly seen foraging in fields throughout the islands.

Amongst the common migrants is one of the smallest passerines – the goldcrest – which only measures about 9cm/3½ins and weighs a mere 5 gms. It is difficult to believe that the tiny, fragile-looking goldcrest feeding in Shetland gardens at this time of year has flown across the North Sea, returning from its breeding grounds in the coniferous forests of Scandinavia. It is an energetic restless little bird, constantly flitting from perch to perch and flicking its wings. The goldcrest takes its name from the lemon-yellow patch edged with black on the crown. In the male the centre of this patch is a deep orange and these feathers can be raised into a small crest when the bird is displaying. Both sexes have olive-green upperparts with two white bars and a black band on the wings, and buff underparts. The eyes appear large and dark, an effect enhanced by a surrounding pale circle of feathers which give this little bird a surprised look. Goldcrests are insect eaters so migrants must spend a considerable amount of daylight searching for suitable prey in order to obtain sufficient energy. Often these charming little birds are heard before they are seen, having a distinctive high-pitched 'zee zee' call note which betrays their presence in thick cover.

Hedgehogs are looking for suitable places to hibernate. During autumn the cooler temperatures and shortage of food cause them to become less and less active.

Hedgehog

However a warmer period can extend activity into late autumn and, even during the coldest months, hedgehogs may wake up for short periods. In Shetland the lack of prolonged periods of frost and low temperatures probably means that hedgehogs do not experience long spells of hibernation. Food reserves are stored under the skin in the form of two types of fat. White fat is widely distributed thoughout the body but large amounts of brown fat are also stored around the neck and shoulders. The brown fat reserves are essential for raising body temperatures back to normal when the animal rouses itself from hibernation. Hedgehogs build themselves winter nests of dry leaves with interwoven grass which forms a tightly-packed weatherproof, insulating layer around the animal. During hibernation the body temperature decreases to that of the surrounding environment but falls no lower than freezing point.

During the second half of October, and into November, grey seals haul on out on inaccessible isolated beaches to give birth to their pups. The main pupping areas are around Fetlar, along the west side of the North Mainland, around the Vee Skerries, Papa Stour and on small islets north of the Out Skerries. The females come ashore about a day before they give birth. Newly-born grey seal pups are clad in dense white furry coats and weigh around 14kg/31lb. Immediately after birth the female repeatedly sniffs at her pup so that she can recognise its scent. The pups are suckled on a very fatty nutrient-rich milk and gain about 2kg/4½lb a day, trebling their birth weight by the end of the 16-18 day suckling period to around 45kg/100lb. Most of the increase is around the girth so the pups become increasingly rotund as a thick layer of blubber forms beneath the skin as a food store and insulation.

Whilst the pups are fattening up the female grey seals are losing weight at a rate of around 4kg/9lb a day. At the end of the suckling period a female grey seal has lost a total of about 65kg/145lb. After lactation the females become sexually receptive and mate with the bulls, which have now taken up territories on the breeding beaches. The fertilised egg does not implant for two or three months so that the seal pups are born at the same time next year, the gestation period only being nine months. The females then return to the sea to replenish their dwindling food reserves, leaving their fat pups behind. The pups' thick white coats provide excellent insulation on land but are prone to rapid waterlogging so these young seals must moult into grey pelages before entering the sea at about 21 days old.

The dominant bulls make their way up the beaches when the first pups are born and take up territories amongst the suckling females. Grey seal bulls are sexually mature at six years old but cannot obtain a territory on the breeding beaches until they are about ten. Size is an important factor in holding a territory and successful bulls weigh between 200-350kg/440-770 lb. These large beachmasters generally maintain their positions amongst neighbouring territory-holders by threat displays. However, if a confrontation does occur it is a noisy bloody affair as the rivals savagely bite at each others head and neck. Most of the encounters are between the beachmasters and smaller non-established males who are quickly seen off. The large size of the dominant grey seal bulls enables them to stay ashore without feeding for several weeks. The females are only receptive once they have weaned their pups so the bulls' time ashore overlaps with that of several females. The largest bulls may mate with more than a dozen partners. However, the males pay a price for this prolonged and stressful breeding season, rarely living longer than twenty five years whilst females can reach the age of thirty five.

In autumn common frogs need to find places in which to spend the winter months. Some males bury themselves in the mud at bottom of ponds, making occasional visits to the surface during milder spells. Although frogs have lungs, they can also absorb oxygen through their thin skins so can remain underwater for long periods. Other males, and most females,

Butterfish

choose a sheltered spot such as inside a stone wall or at the bottom of a heap of vegetation. As air and sea temperatures decrease many inter-tidal organisms disappear from the rocky shore. Some die, having reproduced and completed their life cycles. Others move further down the shore or into deeper water. Sedentary animals, such as beadlet anemones and limpets, have little choice but to remain on the shore but often move into more sheltered crevices. Although anemones appear immobile they can actually inch their way along on their bases using muscular fibres. Crabs and many species of small inshore fish seek out deeper waters but female butterfish remain. They shelter under a stone or in a crevice, curling themselves around their clusters of eggs. During the winter the eggs hatch into planktonic larvae which drift out to sea for several months before returning to inshore waters.

A few species of moth continue to be observed into this month such as dark swordgrass, red swordgrass, beautiful golden Y, brindled ochre and angle shades. The latter is a particularly distinctive moth,

Angle shades moth

75

having long narrow forewings with toothed margins. In the central area of each yellow-brown forewing there is a prominent reddish triangle containing a V-shaped marking. There is also a raised crest on the thorax, obvious when the moth is at rest. Angle shades fly at night and are attracted to both sugar and light. They are migratory but, the presence of pupae in late autumn, suggests that some may be locally-bred. The eggs are laid on a wide variety of plants including dock, chickweed, bramble and ivy. The moth overwinters as a larvae which is either brownish or yellowish-green in colour with a white-dotted line running longitudinally.

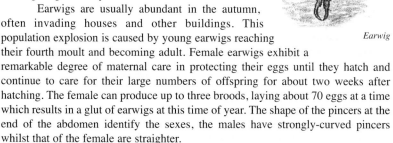

Earwig

Earwigs are usually abundant in the autumn, often invading houses and other buildings. This population explosion is caused by young earwigs reaching their fourth moult and becoming adult. Female earwigs exhibit a remarkable degree of maternal care in protecting their eggs until they hatch and continue to care for their large numbers of offspring for about two weeks after hatching. The female can produce up to three broods, laying about 70 eggs at a time which results in a glut of earwigs at this time of year. The shape of the pincers at the end of the abdomen identify the sexes, the males have strongly-curved pincers whilst that of the female are straighter.

Deciduous trees and shrubs prepare for winter by losing their leaves in order to conserve water during the winter. Autumn colours are created when the tree begins to withdraw valuable chemicals from its leaves. As the chlorophyll begins to break down the red and yellow pigments become visible. A sudden sharp frost heightens the intensity of colour.

Many of the plants flowering in September continue into October. During mild autumns the seeds of annual 'weeds', such as common chickweed, groundsel, red dead nettle and shepherd's purse, continue to germinate and grow. Perennials conserve food stores in stems and roots and generally die back in the autumn, often leaving a rosette of basal leaves which are ready to grow in the spring.

At the time of year that most species are ending their reproductive cycle alder trees are just starting theirs. On mature trees next year's catkins are growing on the twigs along with cones. In Shetland alders will grow successfully when introduced to wet areas with some shelter. The roots produce nodules containing nitrogen-fixing bacteria which can convert atmospheric nitrogen directly into soluble nitrates thus enriching the soil.

During autumn the familiar mushroom and toadstool fruiting bodies of many different species of fungi appear. Fungi are neither plants or animals as their cells

Field Mushrooms

possess characteristics of both groups. The fruiting bodies are the visible form of the fungus but, beneath the soil, are the ramifying fungal threads or *mycelia*. At this time of year the mycelia form a small knob which pushes up through the soil and expands to form a stem and cap. Beneath the cap, arranged radially, are thin plate-like gills which produce spores. As the fruiting body matures the spores are ejected from the gills and dispersed by the wind.

Fungi belonging to the family *Hygrophoracea* or wax caps are very common on grassland pasture. As the name suggests, this group of fungi have thick caps which feel greasy or waxy to the touch. the gills often run down into the stout stem and many species tend to blacken as they mature. A common species is the meadow wax cap, *Hygrocybe pratensis*, which is a delicate buffish-ochre and can grow to a diameter of 8cm/3ins. The scarlet hood has a vivid blood-red cap whilst the parrot wax cap changes colour as it matures. When the fruiting body first appears, the cap is coloured bright green by a thick film which protects the fungus from desiccation or damage. As the toadstool develops, the glutinous covering retreats to the perimeter of the cap and the centre turns yellowish or reddish, finally showing tinges of purple. The stem of this colourful fungus remains greenish-yellow shading into a darker green near the cap

Wax caps are edible but field mushrooms, *Agaricus campestris*, are the most widely eaten species in Shetland. They are particularly common in horse-grazed pastures or where the grass is regularly mown or grazed. Young field mushrooms have a smooth whitish cap beneath which are pale pink gills. The gills turn gradually pinkish-brown and then dark brown as the mushroom matures. The flesh is white and the surface of the cap peels back easily but, if in doubt of identification, the rule is to leave well alone.

By the end of October the hours of darkness are increasing as the Shetland year moves into winter.

—— IN ——
November

November's sky is chill and drear,
November's leaf is red and sear.

Sir Walter Scott

The last month of autumn is often grey, wet and windy as a series of Atlantic depressions track over the islands. Nature is in retreat in face of colder weather and shortening daylight hours. The remaining leaves on the trees, usually blackened and shredded by gales, flutter in ragged pennants from the increasingly bare boughs and twigs. However all seasons have their compensations. On dark calm nights the familiar star constellations wheel into view – Orion, the fuzzy cluster of the Pleiades, the angular outline of the Plough and the sprawling W of Cassiopeia. These nights can also bring spectacular displays of the aurora borealis or northern lights, also known as the 'merry dancers' in Shetland.

These surreal light displays are caused by fast moving streams of charged particles, emitted from the sun, which are attracted to the poles of the earth. As the particles pass through the earth's atmosphere they react with the magnetic field to produce light. The aurora usually begins as a greenish glow close to the northern horizon which may develop into amazing arcs, curtains and beams of light pulsating across the sky in colours ranging through yellowish-green to pink and crimson. One memorable display we witnessed started as a swirl of light which began to glow and twist into a pale green inverted question mark shape. Overhead, arcs and ribbons of light began to unfurl and twist like a rippling curtain of light. The rays swept around the north eastern sky like a celestial lighthouse then suddenly intensified into a brighter green interspersed with tongues of dull pink. The dancing, shifting ever-changing streamers gradually changed to deep crimson. Then, as if a dimmer switch had been operated, the beams began to lose their intensity and merged back into the sky.

At this time of the year the main priority for birds is finding sufficient food in the decreasing hours of daylight. Many species put on an extra layer of sub-cutaneous fat and, during spells of extremely wet windy or cold weather, it may be more efficient to use up some of this reserve rather than expending valuable energy looking for scarce sources of food. Late migrants will have their energy reserves considerably depleted so it is crucial that they can find food quickly. The condition of birds' feathers at this time of year is also vitally important. During cold weather the plumage is fluffed up so that air, warmed by body heat, is trapped within the feathers and provides added insulation. Small birds, such as wrens, are most vulnerable to the cold as their tiny bodies have a high surface to volume ratio and quickly lose heat.

By November garden birds can be provided with supplementary feeding. Any bird table should be sited away from cover, fences or walls to prevent predation by domestic cats. The best time to provide food is in the morning as the birds are most active in the early part of the day. All kinds of kitchen scraps are suitable, especially foods rich in fats and carbohydrates such as bread, cake, biscuits, cooked potato, rice and pasta along with grains and seeds.

Cold weather often brings bird visitors from further north to Shetland gardens and areas with tree or shrub cover. Redpolls are regularly recorded, the commonest being those of the northern race, *Carduelis flammea*, or mealy redpoll. Redpolls are small finches, related to the twite and linnet, with distinctive red foreheads set off by a black chin. Mealy redpolls, which breed in birch forests in Scandinavia, are larger, paler and greyer above with whiter wing-bars and rumps than those of other races.

A more colourful garden visitor at this time of the year is the striking waxwing. These beautiful starling-sized birds are unmistakable with pinkish-brown plumage set off by a bold sweeping crest, black bib and facial mask. The tail has a bright yellow tip with rich chestnut feathers underneath, whilst the tips of the secondary feathers have bright red blobs as though they had been dipped in sealing wax. These contrast with the bright yellow and white of the primary wing feathers. Waxwings are irregular visitors from the coniferous forests of Scandinavia and Northern Russia which appear in Britain when the berry crops in their breeding areas are insufficient to support the population. Their preferred food is rowan berries but they will take the fruit of various other shrub species, often stripping entire bushes before moving on in their ceaseless search for berries.

Waxwing

Glaucous and Iceland gulls are winter visitors from the Arctic, often being recorded from the area around Lerwick harbour. Both species, adults and immatures, can be distinguished from the resident herring and black-backed gulls by the absence of any dark markings on the wings and tail. Adult glaucous gulls vary in size, the largest being comparable to a great black-backed gull. The mantle and wings are pale grey, showing white wing tips in flight, and the underparts white. During the winter the head and chest are streaked with brown. Immatures have streaked brown and white plumage with whitish wing tips and pale dark-tipped beaks. This species has a circum-polar breeding distribution and the birds reaching Shetland are mainly from Greenland and around the Barent Sea. Iceland gulls are smaller and slimmer with longer narrower wings which, at rest, project well beyond the tail feathers. Most probably come from the east Greenland population.

During November whooper swan numbers peak with several hundred on freshwater lochs all over the islands. The largest flock is found on the Loch of

Spiggie which was purchased by the RSPB in 1979 to provide a protected area for overwintering whooper swans. These large elegant birds arrive from Iceland to spend the winter in small family parties. Each group, consisting of a pair along with last summer's offspring, defend a feeding territory within the loch. The adults are readily distinguished from mute swans by the long straight neck, yellow and black bills and trumpeting clarion-like calls. The cygnets are grey-brown with pale greyish bills and the percentage of juveniles within the flocks provides an indicator of breeding success. The swans feed mainly on water plants, upending to reach submerged waterweed, and theirs are a familiar autumn and winter sound.

Long-eared owls are autumn migrants but a few overwinter in the islands in areas with plantations or wooded gardens. During the daytime they roost in dense tree cover, their beautiful greyish-brown barred plumage providing excellent camouflage. The 'long ears' are tufts of feathers which can be raised to make the bird look larger and more menacing. They hunt nocturnally over open ground, using acute hearing to pin-point sounds made by small rodents. Pellet analysis has shown that long-eared owls overwintering in Shetland feed mainly on mice. Owl species are not breeding residents in Shetland due to the lack of suitable woodland habitat and, in the case of moorland species, the absence of small mammals such as field voles. In Orkney areas of moorland and rough pasture have breeding short-eared owls which specialise on populations of the indigenous Orkney vole.

In autumn, mountain hares moult out of their grey-brown coats into white winter pelts. Those resident in Shetland belong to the Scottish race and therefore undergo an almost complete moult. The process is triggered by the shortening hours of daylight and the cooler temperatures. White hairs first appear on the underparts, gradually covering the flanks until the last parts remaining brown are along the backbone and the outer parts of the ears and face. The ear tips always remain black. The winter coat gives the hares a very furry appearance as the long white guard hairs extend beyond the other hairs of the pelt thus increasing the thickness and insulation qualities of the coat. In the Arctic and mountain regions of Britain the white coat camouflages the animals in snowy conditions. However in Shetland these white/brown hares often contrast conspicuously with the sombre moorland backdrop. At this time of year they feed mainly on heather and grass stems, sheltering in the lee of peat banks or in burrows during harsh weather.

Along the seashore many organisms have completed their breeding cycles but the approach of winter stimulates reproduction in some species such as limpets. Influenced by the decrease in temperature and the increased incidence of wave shock on rocky shores, male and female limpets spawn, the eggs and sperm being released into the sea. The fertilised eggs develop into tiny free-swimming larvae, which, after a few days, settle on rocks, in rock pools and in crevices on the middle and upper shore. This new flush of life is easily missed though as the juvenile limpets are less than 1mm in diameter.

Limpets

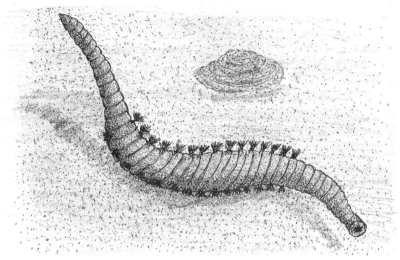

Lugworm

On sandy shores and mud flats lugworms are also breeding. The male worms shed sperm synchronously and fertilisation takes place inside the females' burrows. The eggs hatch into very small larvae which remain in the sand and develop into tiny worms. In order to avoid accidentally eating their offspring the entire lugworm population stops feeding until these minute worms have dispersed. The juveniles are transported by the tide to silty areas further up the shore where they form an important food source for small waders.

Many freshwater organisms employ various strategies to survive the winter. Pondweeds and water milfoils produce winter buds which become detached from the plant and sink into the mud at the bottom of the pond. In spring these buds start to develop into new plants. Water fleas, tiny crustaceans, produce a small quantity of eggs in a brood pouch which remains on the bottom of the pond. The specially thickened walls of the pouch can even withstand freezing and the eggs hatch into a new generation of water fleas in the spring. Some freshwater snails and worms can also survive cold conditions by burrowing into the mud. Protozoa, tiny one-celled animals, can enter a state of suspended animation by forming a protective freeze-resistant cyst around themselves. These cysts can remain viable for years, the organism's becoming active again when conditions improve.

During the early part of the month a few flowering plants can still be found such as marsh ragwort, autumnal hawkbit, prickly sow thistle, yarrow, creeping buttercup and the occasional red campion. Weeds such as common chickweed, red dead nettle, groundsel and shepherd's purse often persist into early winter. These species are quick-growing annuals which can rapidly colonise disturbed ground. The seeds germinate after the autumn rains and the developing plants

Shepherd's Purse

81

can withstand the first frosts.

As November progresses the Shetland countryside becomes increasingly browner as the vegetation withers and is blasted by gales. Evergreens provide most of the remaining shades of green, the term applying to all trees and shrubs where leaves remain on the branches during the winter months. The word is often associated with coniferous trees although several broad-leaved trees and shrubs are also classified as evergreen.

There are no native coniferous trees in Shetland but several species have been introduced with varying degrees of success. During the mid-1950s the Forestry Commission established experimental conifer plantations, mainly of sitka spruce and lodgepole pine, at several sites on the Mainland. Conifers

Skeletonised Leaf

do not grow particularly well in the islands, being susceptible to browning and needle loss from wind-blown salt spray. Sitka spruce only achieve a third of their normal lifespan here and are also vulnerable to attack by aphids, which multiply rapidly in the absence of resident populations of insect-eating birds. However existing coniferous plantations provide valuable habitats and shelter for wildlife and both lodgepole pine and larch survive reasonably well.

Conifers can retain their needles throughout the winter as the long thin shape of these specially adapted leaves cuts down water loss. The needles also contain little sap thus lessening the problems of freezing and are covered in a waxy watertight layer. The arrangement of needles on the twig is a useful aid to identifying different species. Fir-needles are blunt-tipped and grow individually whilst pine needles often grow in pairs, wrapped together by a papery scale at the base of the leaves. Spruce either have pointed four-sided leaves, like the Norway spruce, or have flattened needles but all have peg-like projections on the young shoots.

As November ends the natural calendar enters the last month of the Shetland year and the first month of winter.

—— IN ——

December

Tis the year's midnight
The sun is spent and his flashes
Send forth light squibs, no constant rays
The world's whole sap is sunk.

John Donne

At the winter solstice this month the sun climbs above the horizon for less than six hours. The short winter days often bring little sunshine due to smothering grey blankets of thick cloud accompanying depressions from the North Atlantic. Occasionally the grey-blue curtain parts sufficiently to allow fitful rays of sunlight to illuminate the sombre landscape and some days may feel unseasonably mild. However, December weather is often cold, dominated by the polar air masses to the north of the islands. The month brings the traditional celebrations of Christmas and New Year and, by the end of the festivities, the daylight hours are on the increase once more and the trough of the year is past.

Several species of duck, including mallard, tufted, goldeneye, pochard and teal overwinter on freshwater lochs in Shetland. Mallard are resident breeding birds but the local population is increased by birds from further north. The mallard is the most widely distributed and common species of duck in the northern hemisphere. They belong to the group of dabbling ducks which upend to feed on water plants and aquatic invertebrates. Teal feed in the same manner, the male being readily identified by the small size and Sienna-red head with a distinctive yellow-bordered eyestripe curving down to the nape of the neck. If disturbed, teal are capable of a near vertical take-off as they spring into the air. This species is a regular passage migrant and winter visitor to Shetland with a few breeding pairs.

Small numbers of shoveler, another species of dabbling duck, also overwinter in the islands with a few pairs remaining to breed. Even in poor light conditions both drake and duck are unmistakable due to the large spatulate bill, longer than the head, which gives this duck its common name. Although the shoveler is smaller than the mallard this huge bill gives it a heavier-looking chunkier appearance. The male has a green head, bright chestnut flank patch, white breast and black back and stern. The bill is a very efficient sieve containing fine comb-like plates which extract animal and plant material from the shallow muddy waters in which it feeds.

Tufted, goldeneye and pochard are diving ducks. Tufted and goldeneye feed on insects, shellfish and crustacea, whilst pochard are herbivorous, feeding on stoneworts and pondweeds. The male tufted duck is easily identified by its drooping crest and piebald plumage. The female is browner, with paler markings underneath and has a shorter crest. Goldeneye females are more colourful than the females of most other ducks, having a reddish-brown head, white collar and grey back. The male goldeneye has a dark head with a white blob behind the bill, dark back with white markings, and white underparts. Goldeneye have

Male Shoveler

distinctive high-peaked heads and are tireless divers. Although frequently seen on freshwater they belong to the group of diving sea ducks which includes eiders, scoters and long-tailed duck.

Pochards mainly breed in Russia with a few hundred pairs resident in eastern England. In Shetland they are passage migrants and winter visitors. The male has a chestnut-red head and neck, greyish white body and black breast whilst the duller female has a black bill with a clearly marked blue band. Winter flocks often consist predominantly of one sex as the males leave the northern breeding grounds before the females. By the time that the females arrive some lochs may be full of males and the females will continue further south to winter. Even where the flocks consist of both sexes male pochards tend to feed further from the shore in deeper water than the females, thus reducing competition between the sexes.

The third group of ducks, the sawbills, consist of three species of fish-eaters – smew, goosander and red-breasted merganser. The latter is a passage migrant, winter visitor and breeding resident whilst the smew is a vagrant and the goosander, an uncommon and irregular winter visitor to Shetland. Red-breasted mergansers are almost entirely marine outside the breeding season, favouring sheltered bays and voes where they dive to catch their prey. Mergansers are slimly built, the body shape more akin to that of a grebe or shag than a duck. Males in breeding plumage have a greenish crested head, white collar, tortoiseshell breast and grey flanks whilst the female has a brown head and crest, whitish throat and brown-grey body.

Rock doves are commonly seen during winter feeding in stubble fields. Ancestors of domesticated pigeons, the pure rock dove can be identified by the pale blue-grey back with two clear black wing- bars, and a contrasting white rump. The head and neck are darker grey with a glossy purple-green neck patch. They breed along the cliffs, but visit arable land, especially stubble fields, to feed. Wood pigeons are less common in Shetland being recorded as passage migrants with a few pairs breeding. Small numbers of collared doves have also colonised mature gardens mainly in Lerwick, Scalloway and Brae. Originally only breeding in Turkey and the Balkans, collared doves first bred in Britain in 1955, arriving in Shetland in 1965.

The twite or *lintie* also feeds on stubble fields in winter. The twite is a small finch, closely related to the linnet, mainly found in north-west Scotland, Orkney and Shetland. In Europe, the twite only breeds in Britain and western Norway, the British population being of international importance. In Shetland, these small finches are absent from arable areas during the summer, nesting on grassy cliffs and banks along the coast. During the autumn and winter months they form foraging flocks which visit crofts and farms, favouring weedy fields with abundant seeds. Twite have tawny streaked plumage, long forked tails and yellow bills. Males can be distinguished by their pink rumps. The flight is undulating, usually accompanied by a musical twittering as the birds take to the wing, and the call note is a very characteristic nasal twanging 'chweek'.

Wrens are also resident in Shetland, although they are particularly susceptible to prolonged periods of very hard weather. Many live along rocky shorelines where they creep mice-like around the boulders searching for insects. This behaviour earns the bird its apt Faroese name of *músabródir* which means 'brother to the mouse'. The small size and short cocked tail is diagnostic and the commonest call note is a hard rattling sound although the loud warbling song may be heard during the winter. Wrens are also found inland, especially along the course of burns and in gardens with plenty of cover. They rarely move far from their home area so small island populations have become isolated and developed into sub-species or races which differ with regard to size, colour and song. Sub-species of wren have evolved in Shetland, Fair Isle, the Outer Hebrides and St Kilda. The Shetland race is known as *Troglodytes troglodytes zetlandicus* and is slightly larger and darker than wrens found elsewhere in Britain.

Another small bird, also resident along rocky coastlines throughout the year is the rock pipit or *banks sparrow*. It is a rather nondescript little bird with olive-green streaky plumage and smoky grey tail feathers. Rock pipits favour low rocky shorelines but can also be found living in steep-sided geos. Outwith the breeding season they are generally solitary, feeding in rock crevices or along the strandline. A common prey is the larvae of kelp flies which breed in cast-up decaying seaweed. Another favourite food is the small periwinkle which lives on the upper shore. They are strong fliers and have a loud monosyllabic 'tsip' call note, adaptations for living in an exposed coastal habitat. Sedentary as adults, some juveniles are known to disperse young birds ringed on Fair Isle being found in the Netherlands and in Northern England.

Shetland has few resident garden birds due to the general lack of woodland habitat. The robin, the bird which is associated with Christmas, does not generally breed here but is a common migrant with small numbers over-wintering most years. The birds seen in Shetland are of continental origin, probably from Scandinavia. Black-birds are common, although they only started to breed here in the 1870s. During autumn and winter the resident population is joined by birds from Northern Europe. House sparrows occur around occupied buildings, but the commonest species appearing at

Robin

winter bird tables is the starling. Starlings are found in built-up areas, along the coastline and throughout the countryside. Isolated from their cousins on the mainland, the Shetland population has evolved into a separate race, *Sturnus vulgaris zetlandicus*.

Although the islands are not usually subject to prolonged frost and snow, winter is a testing time for land mammals. Many wild mammals which feed on vegetation reduce their growth rate and eat less which enables them to survive on smaller, less nutritious quantities of food. Changes in appetite and metabolic rate are controlled by the pineal gland which is found in the head. During the hours of daylight this gland produces a chemical, seratonin, which is converted during the night into another chemical, melatonin. As the nights lengthen more melatonin is produced which, in turn, stimulates the production of hormones which control appetite and metabolic rate. These hormones also influence the winter and spring moult of mountain hares and stoats.

December gales often cast up interesting objects such as cuttlebones, the modified internal shells of the common cuttlefish, *Sepia officinalis*, which lives offshore. Cuttlefish belong to the same group of molluscs as squid and octopus and have eight to ten tentacles. The cuttlebone is made up of fine bony plates forming a series of hollow chambers. These chambers, filled with gas, act as a buoyancy device in the living animal.

Cuttlebone

On rocky seashores the brown fucoid seaweeds or wracks are looking increasingly frayed. These seaweeds finish shedding their reproductive cells this month and the fruiting tips of the fronds start to decay and are shed. Depending on the severity of the winter surf, many of the fronds become split and ragged. The shed male and female reproductive cells fuse to form small floating structures capable of growing into new plants. Winter storms often tear away clumps of weed and the resulting areas of bare rock will be rapidly colonised in the spring when the embryo seaweeds settle out on the rocks.

There are few insects around in December but one species of moth emerges at this time of year. The male winter moth, *Operophtera brumata*, is attracted to light and, in mild conditions, hundreds may be recorded. On the evening of 16th December 1995 I recorded over a hundred clinging to the walls and windows of our house. They look rather like small dark-coloured carpet moths. The forewings, which are usually outspread when the moth is at rest, are greyish-brown with darker wavy transverse lines. Female winter moths are virtually wingless. On emerging they crawl up a vertical surface and emit a pheromone to attract the males. After mating, the eggs are laid in sheltered crevices and cracks and, in spring, tiny green caterpillars emerge. These feed and grow, eventually pupating just beneath the surface of the soil, to emerge during December.

In addition to conifers other evergreens commonly seen in Shetland gardens include holly, ivy,

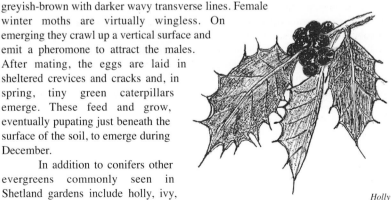

Holly

Hebe and *Olearia*. The first two are indelibly associated with Christmas festivities and, being native to Britain, are most beneficial to wildlife. Holly leaves have a glossy waxy coating which reduces water loss and the lower leaves have sharp prickles to protect the shrub from the attentions of grazing animals. Holly is dioecious, only the fertilised female trees producing the familiar red berries.

Ivy

Ivy is extensively grown in gardens and on walls of buildings but has very rarely colonised any natural habitats and usually does not flower this far north. The leaves are thick with glossy surfaces to resist water loss. As the plant grows upward it produces small climbing roots which grow towards the wall or tree trunk and attach themselves with a cement-like substance. Their only function is attachment, all minerals and water being absorbed by the plant's underground roots. In Britain ivy was widely believed to have magical powers so that its presence in the house would keep away evil forces.

In mild Decembers a few wild flowers may persist such as red campion, prickly sow thistle, groundsel, common chickweed and daisy along with a few garden annuals such as marigold, lobelia, and chrysanthemum. Plant development depends both on temperature and available daylight. Increased average temperatures allow growth and flowering to occur.

Mosses are conspicuous in winter, many of the species growing on rocks and walls producing spores which enable the species to disperse and colonise new habitats. Emerging from the green velvet-like cushions are tiny erect orange stalks, each ending in an oval capsule containing the spores. If a spore lands in a suitable moist shady spot it will grow into a tiny flat green structure bearing both male and female organs. Fertilisation requires water to transmit the male cells to the female organs so mosses can only grow in damp conditions. The fertilised egg then develops into a new moss plant. Rocks and dykes are important habitats for mosses in Shetland but some species prefer to grow on wood. Tree trunks and branches are preferred habitat but old fence posts are also important.

Despite the short hours of daylight there is still a variety of wildlife to be seen in December. As the natural calendar ends we look forward to the familiar sights and sounds which will again mark the seasons of the year in Shetland.

Bibliography

The Natural History of Shetland (1980), Collins, R. J. Berry and J. L. Johnston.

Shetland in Statistics (1994), Shetland Islands Council, Development Department.

Shetland (1975), David & Charles Ltd, James R. Nicolson.

Shetland Official Tourist Guide (1994), Shetland Islands Tourism, text by Joyce J. M. Gammack.

The Flowering Plants and Ferns of the Shetland Islands (1987), The Shetland Times Ltd, Walter Scott & Richard Palmer.

The Natural Environment of Shetland (1974), The Nature Conservancy Council, ed. R Goodier.

Birds and Mammals of Shetland (1955), Oliver & Boyd, L. S. V. and U. M. Venables.

Shetland's Living Landscape (1979), Thule Press, David Spence.

The Shetland Cetacean Reports, The Shetland Cetacean Group.

British Regional Geology - Orkney and Shetland (1976), NERC, Institute of Geological Sciences, W. Mykura.

The Shetland Bird Reports.

The Shetland Entomological Group Reports.

Otters (1994), Colin Baxter Photography Ltd, Bobby Tulloch.

Where to Watch Birds in Shetland (1994), Hugh Harrop.

Shetland's Wild Flowers - A Photographic Guide (1992), The Shetland Times Ltd, D. Malcolm.

National Nature Reserves - leaflets on Hermaness, Noss and Keen of Hamar published by Scottish Natural Heritage.